METHOD OF
Order

METHOD OF
Order

A True Hierarchy of Needs

J. F. Tuckett

WestBow®
PRESS
A DIVISION OF THOMAS NELSON
& ZONDERVAN

WestBow Press books may be ordered through booksellers or by contacting:

WestBow Press
A Division of Thomas Nelson & Zondervan
1663 Liberty Drive
Bloomington, IN 47403
www.westbowpress.com
1 (866) 928-1240

ISBN: 978-1-4908-8905-4 (sc)
ISBN: 978-1-4908-8906-1 (hc)
ISBN: 978-1-4908-8907-8 (e)

Print information available on the last page.

WestBow Press rev. date: 09/01/2015

Dedication

I have served in numerous units in my career; one stands out. I dedicate this book to the Bowie Team—the 39th IBCT (Infantry Brigade Combat Team) HQ, Little Rock, Arkansas.

To past, present, and future members.

1   The Institute of Heraldry, "Shoulder Sleeve Insignia, 39th Infantry Brigade," accessed February 17, 2013, http://www.tioh.hqda.pentagon.mil/Heraldry/ ArmyDUISSICOA/ArmyHeraldryUnit.aspx?u=3663.

Remembering a Soldier

Captain Arthur "Bo" Felder, KIA, Taji, Iraq, 24 April 2004.

Purpose

This book is about understanding God, his ways, and who he is.

This is what the Lord says: "Stand at the crossroads and look; ask for the ancient paths, ask where the good way is, and walk in it, and you will find rest for your souls."

—Jeremiah 6:16 (NIV)

Table of Contents

Foreword

Suicide has become a major topic in military circles for very good reason. The topic has gained a renewed and reinvigorated emphasis in light of complications involving post-traumatic stress symptom manifestations. Another alarming possible trend is young soldiers, never deployed but find themselves in difficult situations and see suicide as a viable option.

I am especially encouraged to see the level of research, thought, and prayer that went into the development of this book. I have personally witnessed a lack of effective leadership too many times in my career as an enlisted soldier and a chaplain. We have all witnessed what appears to be a tendency to have a briefing on suicide prevention and check off a box to say "Look—see, we have done our job" and then act surprised when the suicide numbers rise rather than fall.

Using the seven churches of Asia as the examples was next to genius. The way Maj. Tuckett was able to draw what are obvious (not contrived truths) and examples from these churches and then tying in other Scripture again in obvious, not contrived ways was perfect. The fifteen corroborating examples only lend more support to the thesis of the book. The practical applications are spot-on. I personally teach and preach to all who will listen that everything depends upon relationship. Everyone needs a sense of belonging. Anyone can understand that humility breeds real life. Everyone needs to feel as though they are individually worthy and have value. Everyone needs to understand that they have a responsibility to a larger group. Everyone needs to understand that if there is no focus, there is no finish. The group depends upon the individuals having a collective vision, which must be articulated and encouraged via the leaders. And finally, we must all be true to an original purpose which is connected to the past.

The example of the founding documents of our nation was really eye-opening, and again, it was obvious when pointed out, not contrived. The ultimate tie-in of the twenty-eight-star leadership model is easy to understand. Framing it as a biblical hierarchy of needs is spot-on. I repeat again, it is logical, not contrived. I also thought that Maj. Tuckett articulated the factors of suicide very well in a chart form.

Using a combined faith-based/leadership strategy approach rather than simply a clinical approach will resonate with leaders—and leaders with spiritual moorings especially. I have long believed that our tendency to treat specific problems such as addictions and suicide by *only* focusing on addictions and suicide has been a mistake. We should have been focusing on principles, practices, and character. This approach is along that line.

My hope is that this book will be widely read and then utilized. If chaplains will be the catalysts, presenting this to their commanders as a tool to teach leadership strategy, which will result in fostering an environment that will reduce the scourge of suicide among service members, we will all benefit.

Chaplain John Mark Wheeler,
Captain, 1-151st Cavalry

Preface

This is a personal testimony. No one should think because I have written this book I imply to have leadership figured out. One of the reasons I am able to achieve a level of understanding is due to my past mistakes.

I do not write or speak on behalf of any office, agency, or organization. Namely, I do not write on behalf of the US Army, the Army National Guard, or any unit formerly assigned or the unit of my current assignment. I do not have that authority, nor do I pretend to or imply that I have such authority. This book is not political, tactical, or operational in nature. It does not cover topics of national strategy. This book covers theological and philosophical topics of leadership based in Scripture. I apply these leadership principles to the ongoing problem of suicide that has affected our military and has begun to affect military families in similar ways. As with any new idea, any person can freely accept or reject all or some of the points. This book cites appropriate, unclassified, and open-source information available to the public at large. The Defense Office of Prepublication and Security Review has reviewed this work.

After more than twenty years of combined service and three combat tours in US Marine infantry, US Army National Guard infantry, and cavalry units, I have a deep love for this trade, my regiments, and those with whom I have served. Mutual respect is an impetus for this book. Hopelessness and suicide have visited our ranks. This book can be a lifeline for those who struggle with lack of purpose and meaning. This book outlines some of God's own leadership goals and style. We can borrow God's ways to make them our ways. He shows us his coherent order in his Holy Bible. This order has lain dormant, embedded in Scripture for millennia—until now.

Our sense of belonging from God will unlock this mystery. I codify this new and fresh information in my twenty-eight-star leadership model that I entirely base on Scripture. Take this journey through the seven churches of Revelation with me. See God's coherent order in his plan for your life. God's principles of leadership and followership will act as our guide. God will lead us to hope, purpose, and true meaning.

Acknowledgments

For seeing me through two combat tours and countless training events, I offer my love and gratitude to my beautiful wife, Bevie.

For teaching me the truth of the Lord and for your professional and technical help on this book, I offer my love to my parents, Floyd, an SBC preacher, and Elizabeth.

For editing this work, I would be remiss not to acknowledge my mother, an accomplished English teacher.

For allowing permissions, I offer my special thanks to the following: Barbour Publishing Inc.; Bonnie M. K. Hagerty, PhD, RN; David W. McMillan, PhD; Mindworks Photography; QuickSeries Publishing; Sid Israel Roth and the *Sid Roth's It's Supernatural!* team; Sovereign Grace Publishers Inc.; and The Institute of Heraldry.

Introduction

Obey your leaders and submit to their authority. They
keep watch over you as men who must give an account.
Obey them so that their work will be a joy, not a
burden, for that would be of no advantage to you.

—Hebrews 13:17

This book reveals God's order for our lives, and this coherent structure is new revelation. No secular or religious scholars or lay authors have identified this order. It has lain embedded in Scripture for millennia, dormant. This coherent structure, found in multiple scriptural examples, is new and untouched. Since it is new, this order has not had practical application until now. I will apply it practically in our responsibilities of leadership and identify the sequel effects of subordinate responsibilities we all have. Most importantly, I will apply it in the realm of suicide prevention.

An antidote to suicide is hope. Hope is an expression of faith. Faith develops through evidence for belief. Belief in God creates the phenomenon of sense of belonging from God, building resilience. Resilience during adversity is a known protective factor against suicide. Suicide and hope are not compatible. God's leadership structure builds hope and contentment through a sense of belonging. This journey inspires hope.

We will start this journey in the seven churches of Revelation (Revelation 2–3). The churches and their city names are synonymous. These names in sequential order are Ephesus, Smyrna, Pergamum,

Thyatira, Sardis, Philadelphia, and Laodicea. Ephesus is the first church, and this city will unlock the logic we need to understand the Scripture of the other six cities. The verses of Scripture for each separate church will provide us a central, key lesson and a reward. These lessons and rewards, I have discovered, are entirely new, fresh, and exciting. This is a completely new way to view the churches, if not a new technique to interpret the Bible. Their application will generate contentment in our jumbled and often hectic lives that only Christ can provide.

The rewards we gain in each of the seven churches will construct a leadership model for us. This model will show us how to order our lives and how leaders should lead their organizations. In Chapter 8, I highlight fifteen scriptural examples as proofs that corroborate this claim of discovery of an ancient divine order and structure.

This newly-discovered method of order will enable leaders in any context. This order has use and purpose for any leader or subordinate in any type of organization. To help battle the increased number of suicides plaguing our nation's military, this book will have special meaning. This is one of the principal purposes of this book. The new revelation is important in and of itself, but its application to touch lives in our day in such a profound way trumps any academic knowledge.

The 2012 National Strategy for Suicide Prevention (2012 NSSP) Appendix D identifies eleven groups that statistically are more likely to be in peril of suicide. Members of our armed forces and veterans are in this grouping. No other occupation or career field categorically places a person in a risk threshold. Although there is dispute about this next statistic from the Centers for Disease Control and Prevention (CDC), the point is still relevant, even if potentially artificially high. The CDC estimates veterans account for 20 percent of the suicides in America.[2]

---

2   US Department of Health and Human Services (HHS) Office of the Surgeon General and National Action Alliance for Suicide Prevention. *2012 National Strategy for Suicide Prevention: Goals and Objectives for Action.* Washington, DC: HHS, September 2012, Appendix D, 101, 124.

We can hardly pick up a newspaper or publication that does not touch on this problem of suicide in our nation's military. The US Secretary of Defense, Leon Panetta, spoke to the House Armed Services Committee in July 2012 and described the suicide problem as an epidemic.[3] Now there are even reports that this problem reaches into service member families.

This book can be a lifeline for those who struggle with meaning and purpose and have had ideation of suicide. This book will be relevant for all types of leaders who seek to know God's coherence and structure. Leaders can use this information to combat suicide in their organizations.

There are multiple goals and sub-point objectives attached to each goal in the 2012 NSSP. This book, through the Christian perspective, will specifically address the 2012 NSSP's Goal #1, Objective 1.1, and sub-bullet point two from the national strategy. Faith is a known protective factor against suicide, and I seek to develop this point of resilience to its full potential to save lives.

> 2012 NSSP Goal 1: Integrate and coordinate suicide prevention activities across multiple sectors and settings.
>
> 2012 NSSP Objective 1.1: Integrate suicide prevention into the values, culture, leadership, and work of a broad range of organizations and programs with a role to support suicide prevention activities.
>
> 2012 NSSP Sub-bullet point 2 of Objective 1:1: Faith-based programs[4]

---

3   Kathleen Miller, "Military Faces Suicide 'Epidemic,' Panetta Tells Congress," *Bloomberg Businessweek News From Bloomberg,* July 25, 2012, accessed January 31, 2013, http://www.businessweek.com/news/2012-07-25/military-faces-suicide-epidemic-panetta-tells-u-dot-s-dot-lawmakers.

4   US Department of Health and Human Services (HHS) Office of the Surgeon General and National Action Alliance for Suicide Prevention. *2012 National Strategy for Suicide Prevention: Goals and Objectives for Action.* Washington, DC: HHS, September 2012, 29-30.

Before you depart on your journey through the seven cities, you will need some ground rules for reading through the churches of Revelation. There are multiple valid ways to view these churches and interpret their meanings.

These churches actually existed in the day when the apostle John wrote Revelation, the last book of the Bible. These churches have dispensational meaning. That is to say, a church represents an age or an extended era. The seven church ages are in chronological sequence. The entire greater church age begins on the day of Pentecost, as viewed by many scholars. The entire greater church age ends with the rapture. These are the two bookends of the complete church age.

These seven churches then subdivide the greater church age. From the beginning of the church's inception, it has had a shelf life—a known start and end—defined by God. Although the church is eternal and perpetual, its venue will be in heaven post-rapture when and where the nature of its mission will transform.

John P. Newport, the author of *The Lion and the Lamb,* defines this concept. "Revelation is primarily a forecast of the development of history. This is called the Historicist or (the) Continuous-historical View. Definition: This view affirms that Revelation is a symbolic presentation of the entire course of the history of the Western church from the close of the first century to the end of time."[5]

Another completely valid view used to augment the previous historical and chronological view is that each of these churches simultaneously exists presently and existed formerly. Scripture often gives warnings to all the churches together at one time, so we know this technique is valid.[6] There are a few other ways to view the churches and their interpreted meanings. Scholars write on this in other works. Other scriptural interpretations of the churches may be necessary to understand multiple meanings and their associated truths. We, however, will use the historical approach as we sequentially travel

---

5   John P. Newport, *The Lion and the Lamb: A Commentary On The Book Of Revelation For Today* (Nashville: Broadman Press, 1986), 86.

6   Example: Revelation 2:23

from city to city and visit each church in order to get our central key lesson and our reward. This sequential order is a tenet of this book. I borrow this order to structure my leadership model.

All these churches in ancient times were along a road. If a mail carrier had a bag of letters for delivery, he would start the journey in Ephesus and end it in Laodicea. Each city he would visit along this mail route would be the same city that the sequence in Revelation shows: Ephesus, Smyrna, Pergamum, Thyatira, Sardis, Philadelphia, and Laodicea, all in that order.[7] We will use the same order as we travel, too.

The rewards we attain in each city have to be in this exact same sequence. You cannot skip a city, because you would skip out on the reward. If you did get the reward in the next city, it would not make sense, or it would be unfounded (not rightly earned). Remember, in each city, you also have a lesson to learn that enables you to earn that reward.

The lesson also matures you so you can responsibly use your reward through a practical application inside the context of your God-given gifts. Each reward builds into a culminating reward in the last city. The reward of Laodicea ties all the rewards together. Think of each church's reward as a graduation into the next phase of your journey of leadership development. Skipping ahead will only put you behind. Stay with the program.

At the end of the journey, you will have seven rewards. We will keep track of the sequence of rewards along the way. These seven rewards can build the structure of the rest of your life using God's method that he designed and modeled for us. This order goes back to the Garden of Eden, where God first spoke to Adam and Eve of this coherent structure.

This structure has application in how we interact with everyone we know in any setting. The lives of those we influence as leaders will be

---

7   Jack W. Hayford, Ed., *New Spirit Filled Life Bible,* New King James Version (Nashville: Thomas Nelson Inc., 2002), 1818.

the true beneficiaries. This book and its lessons and rewards are for everyone—leaders and subordinates. We are all both of these.

Before we start our journey, some may ask how the Bible can help or be relevant when it is so old. It helps precisely because it is old. It is a window into God's timeless spirit, and its age is one of the very qualities that enhances its claim of truth. "This is what the Lord says: 'Stand at the crossroads and look; ask for the ancient paths, ask where the good way is, and walk in it, and you will find rest for your souls'" (Jeremiah 6:16).

Jesus is the singular baseline to start our journey. The basis for this newly-discovered structure is completely in Scripture. An ancient biblical model of leadership is now discovered, codified, and no longer dormant.

The Method of Order—Road Map for our Journey

The reward of Ephesus leads us to the reward of Smyrna, which leads us to the reward of Pergamum, which leads us to the reward of Thyatira, which leads us to the reward of Sardis, which leads us to the reward of Philadelphia, which leads us to the reward of Laodicea.

The process follows:

1. The Ephesus model reveals the central lesson in each city.

2. The lesson prepares us for the reward.

3. The rewards combined in sequence are the constructs of the *method of order.*

4. The stages or constructs of the *method of order* build the twenty-eight-star leadership model.

    •   The twenty-eight-star leadership model has application in general leadership and suicide prevention. The primary utility of the twenty-eight-star leadership model in suicide prevention is to set the spiritual conditions so a person never entertains suicide as a viable option in life.

- The *method of order* reveals the mystery of an interconnected coherence throughout Scripture across many hundreds of years. This quality is not within the scope of mortal ability and points to a singular author. This strengthens the apology of the Messianic position.

CHAPTER 1

The Churches: Ephesus

Dominion and awe belong to God; he establishes
order in the heights of heaven.

—Job 25:2

Welcome to Ephesus

We will start our journey from here. We have seven cities to visit.
There will be lessons and rewards in each city we visit. The seven
rewards will build the framework of God's method of order for our
lives.

I joined the USMC in 1988 and reported to my first duty location
at MCRD (Marine Corps Recruit Depot), San Diego, California, in
August of that year. All the new recruits were placed into a reception
unit for about a week to allow the roster to fill enough to constitute a
training battalion. Just a pair of running shoes and one set of utilities
consisting of a pair of pants, a shirt, and a hat were issued to us. At
no point during this week were we ever referred to as Marines. We
looked terrible and sloppy.

Our pants may or may not have been the correct size; our hats were
pulled down by our ears, and our utility shirts did not have the eagle,
globe, and anchor on the front left pocket. Anyone from a mile away
knew we were the next gaggle of recruits-in-waiting for a training

battalion assignment. We could not march, and the troop-handlers in charge of us pretty much gave up on calling any cadence.

The troop-handlers' main responsibility was to shepherd—but mostly herd—us for the next week so that we would arrive to our training battalion alive and not tear too much up in the process. It was evident to everyone involved we were mostly a liability to the USMC at this point in our careers. We had not proven ourselves in any tests, and our sense of belonging was nil. Nevertheless, that was about to change in a profound way. We have a very profound lesson forthcoming in Ephesus, too.

We will look at a few concepts from the scriptural excerpt dealing with the church in Ephesus—the lessons and the reward. The central lesson is the idea of testing, being tested, and their effect on us. The reward portion is a sense of belonging.

Let us get going and meet the people in our first church! Before we start our hellos, you will need to unpack your faith and keep it handy.

- Faith: belief, an assent of the mind to such matters, the reality of which depends upon testimony (Dictionarium Britannicum 1736).[8]

- "Now faith is the substance of things hoped for, the evidence of things not seen" (Hebrews 11:1 NKJV). [9]

Not all definitions of the same word are equal. There are definitions of faith that are near opposite in meaning to these two examples. There are postmodern definitions that grind the axe of secularism. These claim that faith is blind, requiring no proof. This book is a testimony of evidence to inspire faith.

---

8   N. Bailey, Comp., *Dictionarium Britannicum: Or a more compleat Etymological English Dictionary Than any Extant Second Edition* (London: Lamb under the Royal Exchange, 1736), between 4N and 4O.

9   Jack W. Hayford, Ed., *New Spirit Filled Life Bible*, New King James Version (Nashville: Thomas Nelson Inc., 2002), 1741.

Belief in God requires faith. Some have faith to believe; some do not. The question of belief is not avoidable.

Revelation 2:1–7 was written to the church in Ephesus:

> To the angel of the church in Ephesus write: These are the words of him who holds the seven stars in his right hand and walks among the seven golden lampstands: I know your deeds, your hard work and your perseverance. I know that you cannot tolerate wicked men, that you have tested those who claim to be apostles but are not, and have found them false. You have persevered and have endured hardships for my name, and have not grown weary. Yet I hold this against you: You have forsaken your first love. Remember the height from which you have fallen! Repent and do the things you did at first. If you do not repent, I will come to you and remove your lampstand from its place. But you have this in your favor: You hate the practices of the Nicolaitans, which I also hate. He who has an ear, let him hear what the Spirit says to the churches. To him who overcomes, I will give the right to eat from the tree of life, which is in the paradise of God.

The Foundation: Sense of Belonging—Stage One

You do not have to study group or community psychology long before you learn about a sense of belonging. It is a foundational aspect of community. Secular scholars have defined this concept at length. Secular scholars have also placed sense of belonging into a hierarchy among other needs that are essential in an orderly society.

There are components of truth in secular views that cross over into biblical truth. I, for the first time, will define sense of belonging through Scripture that has lain embedded, dormant—until now. The scripture of the Ephesian church will lead the way on our journey toward the destination—a sense of belonging.

Every group has discrete criteria that define its existence. A first cause, an authority source, must define and offer the criteria. Potential members must view these criteria as legitimate to justify the formation of an entity or organization. Some have entry, and some cannot. Maybe some choose not to enter. A selection process screens potential members. More stringent entrance criteria will make the organization more exclusive. It is a lot easier to be a starter for flag football than to earn a starting position for the Dallas Cowboys.

Within the context of a group, there is an internal hierarchy of members. Only one person can be the CEO. Additional refinement of criteria is the basis for this inner hierarchy. The organization establishes an order of merit to structure its members into strata of internal positions based upon abilities and measured capability.

The individuals in the group must recognize this structure as valid and necessary. The group, in return, must value the individual member. Defining criteria at the outset establishes the discrete boundaries of the organization and internal graduations of hierarchy.

The scope of its existence depends upon viable criteria people view as legitimate. The leaders of the group must then ensure that the organization continues to exist in the scope of its predetermined purpose. The organization must have discipline in this regard.

Just as there must be a mechanism in the group to monitor gates of entry, the group must actively ensure that its identity of purpose perpetuates itself. The people must have discipline to stay on message. The group and its members must protect their own defined boundaries through unity and continuity. Their meaning is gained through a common purpose. This will establish a shared history that transcends each generation or cycle of members. Their legacy is their shared history.

Purpose, traditions, customs, etc. project their identity. Their identity projects their essence—their *raison d'être*. Each generation or cycle of members and current components of the group must guard these aspects to ensure that a shared history connects all the members.

Without a legacy of a common history, the group's identity and purpose will be in continuous flux. Members will define the group's meaning in their own way, confusing the entire purpose of the group's existence. Past members will not recognize the intent of the new group, even though the group is the same—but in name only. People outside of the group will interpret this flux as chaos. The value, meaning, and pride of membership will diminish.

All these points together comprise a sense of belonging. A sense of belonging is an idea composed of seven components that I list below. I derive this list from Scriptures about the church of Ephesus. Seven sequential stages (constructs) generate a sense of belonging in a group. In this instance, the group is the church. They are as follows:

The Ephesus Model

1. There must be an agent of first cause. This agent must have valid authority to offer definitive criteria that will establish the identity and intentions of a group.

2. Potential members must recognize the criteria and their giver as legitimate and coherent in order to define a discrete entity of purpose. The group must have a common set of core values that will apply to all the members. These are the foundations of their hope.

3. You must have members. They must collectively operate inside the predetermined scope of purpose identified at the start by the giver through defining criteria. The members must be loyal to the group and its founder or founding authority. The group must struggle through adversity—a problem or threat—to solidify the bond. This brings the group to life with spirit of personality.

4. The group must value its individual members. (A mob shares constructs 1–3, not 4–7.)

5. The agent of first cause with authority and empowered members must retain discretion to make corrective actions so the group will stay on message and mission. This will retain the charter identity of the group.

6. The agent of first cause with authority and empowered members must shepherd the group into success. This will be the realization of a fulfilled hope.

7. A legacy translates into a shared history.

Proof in Scripture for the Seven Constructs of the Ephesus Model

1. Jesus was the agent of first cause (Revelation 2:1–2). Jesus caused the churches to exist. He held the seven stars (symbol for angels, Revelation 1:20). This symbolizes his authority to define the church's coherent boundaries, purpose, and meaning. Jesus inspired the charter as its sponsor. This is a top-down invitation of acceptance, an offer of integration. The holiness and righteousness of God are the source of the criteria that defined the church as an entity of purpose.

2. The church of Ephesus has members; therefore, we know they recognized and submitted to the holy authority of God. They became stakeholders in God's purpose. This is bottom-up reciprocal acceptance of God and his laws.

3. They loyally persevered in deeds of hard work (Revelation 2:2) in the name of Christ, solidifying the bonds in the church. The bonds expressed their collective spirit of personality.

4. The church of Ephesus placed value on their members. We know this, because they did not tolerate wickedness (Revelation 2:2), so they must have honored righteousness. In addition, Jesus commended them for their work ethic. For whom did they work? They worked to support people. Ninety-nine percent of all organizations do this.

5. They also demonstrated bonds of mutual discipline as they confronted wickedness and strived to stay on message (Revelation 2:2).

6. Jesus commended them for perseverance and enduring hardships for his name, and they did not grow weary (Revelation 2:3). This success gave them credibility and was

a realization of hope they first had from stage two. (Without hope, they never would have joined the church or any organization.)

7. However, they struggled with continuity of purpose (Revelation 2:4–5), stage seven in the Ephesus model. They had an internal problem. Their fractures were from internal stress, not any external threats. The Son of Man, Jesus, instructed them to remember the heights they once had. The church in Ephesus betrayed its original love (Revelation 2:4–5). Their purpose of meaning shown by these members was not the same purpose of meaning the charter members once knew. Their common history diminished as their identity changed into something outside of the original intent of the agent of first cause (Jesus). Their charter intent morphed. This is a chaotic trend.

These verses covering Ephesus contain all seven components of a scriptural sense of belonging. Stages one through six are positive, and stage seven is a negative example. However, it is a valid example to communicate the idea—perhaps better than a positive example.

The seven stages define the church's mutual sense of belonging from and toward God. The stages also apply to the connections between the collective members and the individual member alike. These are the three dimensions of every sense of belonging. They are top-down, bottom-up, and lateral connections. Order matters.

The Ephesus model has practical use to describe the sense of belonging we experience in our organizations. It follows Scripture and nature.

The Ephesus Model in the Formation of Our Nation

Look at our nation's history through the lens of the Ephesus model for a sense of belonging.

1. Our proto-government wrote the Declaration of Independence as a charter. As the agent of first cause, this proto-government established the criteria we use to define our existence.

2. Fueled by hope, subjects transformed into citizens through these criteria that defined this new nation.

3. As a nation, we have struggled through dark days, especially the early days of the Revolution. Bonds of identity and common purpose require adversity to form and strengthen. This nation has met that requirement. The spirit of our collective personality emerges because of adversity.

4. We value our citizens. Mistreatment from the Crown was the impetus behind the Declaration of Independence in the first place.

5. We remain relevant today, even with an eighteenth-century charter. As a constitutional republic, we have some baseline laws that cannot change and some that can change. For example, we still have a navy, and its ships are not wooden.

6. Our government is comprised of empowered citizens. Birthright leadership spawned stage one in our nation's history. Our nation has enjoyed successes. This is our fulfilled hope from stage two.

7. We continue to exist with the same charter. This perseverance is our shared history with the Greatest Generation and the first generation of Americans.

The Ephesus Model in Everyday Use

Think of the Ephesus model in the context of when you joined a club or organization. The natural flow of the almost subconscious steps are shown in this model for a sense of belonging.

The seven constructs of a sense of belonging through defined short titles and explanation:

1. Invitation: the organization recognizes the individual as a fit for it (top-down).

2. Consideration: the individuals recognize the organization as a fit for them (bottom-up).

3. Entrance: the individual joins in the struggle and loyally supports the goals and shared purpose of the organization in a meaningful way. This expresses the character, personality, or spirit of the group.

4. Acceptance: this is a symbiotic relationship. The organization benefits from the individual, and the individual benefits from the organization.

5. Discipline: the organization can correct course to maintain its original relevance.

6. Commendation: the organization recognizes exceptional individuals for supporting the shared goals of the organization.

7. Identity: unity with continuity will translate into a legacy with meaning and a shared history.

When you became a member of an organization, did you use these main ideas? You were invited. You asked questions about the organization. You decided to join. The organization accepted you as an equal. You maintained its code and requirements. You received recognition and credibility through the organization. You were part of the organization, and the organization was part of you. These are the components of a sense of belonging as defined by Scripture in the Ephesus model.

The seven stages of the Ephesus model culminate in a sense of belonging for the individual because of the collective of individuals. It is a fusion of top-down and bottom-up influences. "Come near to God and he will come near to you" (James 4:8). This is a key lesson of Ephesus, and it will be a recurring theme throughout this book.

Unlocking the Meaning

The Ephesus model is scriptural, and it works with everyday common sense. I have exercised it through some examples to prove this.

The Ephesus model unlocks information. The text of Ephesus (Revelation 2:1–7) provides us the context we need to interpret the meaning of the other six churches. We will use a stage from the Ephesus model in each corresponding city we travel to along this journey.

Smyrna is the second city, and we will use the second stage of the model to understand the text dealing with Smyrna. Each stage will lead us to our lesson, and the lesson will lead us to the reward. Together, the rewards we gain from our lessons will build the *method of order* and subsequently the twenty-eight-star leadership model.

Outline

The Stages of the Ephesus Model—Sense of Belonging

Stage 1: The lesson is the test, and the reward is a sense of belonging.

Stage 2: The lesson is humility, and the reward is life.

Stage 3: The lesson is to know the Word and your job, and the reward is individual worth and value.

Stage 4: The lesson is to have a heart, and the reward is individual responsibility to support the group.

Stage 5: The lesson is to keep focus, and the rewards are rest, companions, protection, and contentment.

Stage 6: The lesson is enablement, and the reward is credibility.

Stage 7: The lesson is not to forget, and the reward is autonomy to lead and create.

Secular View

Secular scholars also define a sense of belonging and capture the essence of its meaning well. I lean on their definitions as I look to Scripture to develop and refine the concept of a sense of belonging.

David W. McMillan and David M. Chavis (1986) propose their definition: "Sense of community is a feeling that members have of belonging, a feeling that members matter to one another and to the group, and a shared faith that members' needs will be met through their commitment to be together (McMillan 1976)."[10]

Bonnie M. K. Hagerty, *et al* (1992) propose their definition: "We have defined sense of belonging as the experience of personal involvement in a system or environment so that persons feel themselves to be an integral part of that system or environment."[11]

---

10   David W. McMillan and David M. Chavis, "Sense of Community: A Definition and Theory," *Journal of Community Psychology,* Vol. 14 (January 1986): 9.

McMillian 1976 refers to an unpublished manuscript of David W. McMillan at George Peabody College for Teachers, Nashville, Tennessee, in the bibliography of "Sense of Community: A Definition and Theory," *Journal of Community Psychology,* Vol. 14 (January 1986).

11   Bonnie M.K. Hagerty, *et al*, "Sense of Belonging: A Vital Mental Health Concept," *Archives of Psychiatric Nursing,* Volume VI, No. 3 (June 1992): 173, accessed February 1, 2013, http://deepblue.lib.umich.edu/bitstream/handle/2027.42/29998/0000365.pdf;jsessionid=A72108C27BC45E9611671A6C664A4E85?sequence=1.

A scriptural sense of belonging shares these same points. Most notably, a sense of belonging is a two-way street. A one-sided relationship is rarely valid.

Scriptural Sense of Belonging: Definition Proposal

God, through nature, his Word, his Spirit, and his church, communicates to his creation a sense of belonging that we accept or reject. This proposed definition attempts to capture the three facets of the phenomenon of sense of belonging. Sense of belonging describes an experience of community where lateral bonds of mutual respect are created by the fusion of (first) top-down acceptance and integration and (second) bottom-up commitment.

Graphical Depiction:
The Fret of Scriptural Sense of Belonging

The Lesson

When I was in high school, we had a club that was self-styled as somewhat antiestablishment. It had two provisions for entrance. First, you had to be a senior. Second, you could not be in any other club, organization, or athletic team on campus. You truly had to be a bum (their terminology). If you were in the math club, you had a choice to make. If you were on the baseball team, you had to quit. Either you were a bum or you were not. The test for entrance was only two questions. Even this organization, of all organizations, had entrance criteria to hold the line on.

Does it seem odd that this church in Ephesus tested others? We do the same things. Our doctors, pilots, lawyers, and welders are tested. Do you want to be on the tenth floor of a building welded by unqualified workers? Every profession or organization has a test of entrance. Subsequent tests order the members once they are accepted.

Nine Examples of Testing

Revelation 2:2 is the specific portion we will focus on for now. This Scripture speaks of how the church was responsible and successfully fulfilled its obligation to test those who claim to have spiritual authority. Testing is a method to identify areas that drift from the charter intent of the organization.

We will look at nine other testing examples shown in the Bible to see how the test had a purpose with an outcome that defined the group or strengthened the bonds inside the group.

1. In Genesis 22:1–19, Abraham passed a test and offered Isaac, his son, as a sacrifice. God stopped Abraham and provided a ram instead. Then God confirmed his promise to Abraham that all the earth would be blessed through him. That is to say, God's identity as a holy, good, caring, and righteous entity would be revealed to all humanity through the Jews.

2. Exodus 20 (Exodus 20:20, specifically) identifies the Ten Commandments as a test to instill fear of God to keep the people from sinning.

3. In Lamentations 3:38–42, Jeremiah pleaded with the people to get them to examine themselves. He wanted them to test themselves. He wanted them to see that they were in rebellion against the Lord. Repentance generates restoration.

4. In Zechariah 13:8-9, God said he would test the people so that they would claim God as their own. God, in return, would claim the people as his own.

5. In Acts 5:1-11, Ananias and Sapphira failed to tell the truth in their collusion. They also failed their individual tests separately when Peter confronted each one, resulting in their immediate death. Then great fear and respect fell upon the church for God and his holy nature.

6. In Acts 18:24-28, Apollos proved that Jesus was the Messiah through the Scriptures to the great benefit of the believers in Achaia.

7. First Timothy 3:8-10 provides criteria for deacon qualifications before serving the church body.

8. First Timothy 5:19 provides criteria for accusations against an elder to prevent vengeful and untrue accusations.

9. First John 4:1-6 provides a test to see if a spirit is the Spirit of God.

God uses a test to establish, coalesce, or define or refine the group and give the group purpose and direction. The test is intentional with a desired outcome. The test is a catalyst to develop individuals within the context of a specified community and its identity. God develops us in the same exact way in our lives. We should expect to prove ourselves periodically for our own benefit and the benefit of our communities. Your community may be your family, church, circle of friends, military unit, or place of employment.

Nine Examples of Testing with Detail

In Genesis 22, God tested Abraham by asking Abraham to offer his son Isaac as a sacrifice. Genesis 22:17-18 reveals the intent of the test or desired outcome that Abraham successfully achieved. All nations to this day receive blessings through Abraham. That is to say, through Abraham, the monotheistic religions of Judaism (first) (Romans 1:16) and Christianity (second) (Romans 11:17) introduce humanity to God. Replete Scriptures substantiate this. A few follow: Genesis 12:1–3, Exodus 19:4–6, Deuteronomy 14:2, Psalm 147:19–20, Isaiah 42:1–6, Isaiah 49:6, Amos 9:11–15, Luke 2:32, Acts 10:45, Acts 11:18, Acts 15:15–18, Acts 28:28, Romans 3:29, Romans 4:1–17, and Galatians 3:14, among others. "He has revealed his word to Jacob, his laws and decrees to Israel. He has done this for no other nation; they do not know his laws" (Psalm 147:19–20).

The Jewish community is one of the oldest (if not the oldest) community in existence, practicing the same religion and tracing its lineage from the present day to Abraham. This is a miracle in itself. The test establishes the foundations for the role of the Jewish community to reveal God to the world and establishes Abraham as the patriarch of the (then) forthcoming Jewish community that is still intact today. Through this test, the identity of the group is defined. Its purpose is articulated and published for all to readily see. It is a kingdom of priests.

John Helton writes,

> The whole earth was covered with thick darkness, and lay plunged in gross ignorance. Only one country, and that of very small extent, knew the true God. In Judah is God known, his Name is great in Israel, elsewhere all mouths were mute in respect to Him, and the hymns of idolatrous solemnities were only invitations to crimes.[12]

In Exodus 20, the Ten Commandments were a test given to the Israelites so that God could reveal himself holy and worthy to precipitate a community with a clear identity around himself. He gave the Ten Commandments as foundational rules for the community to operate with and established himself as its ultimate and rightful holy

---

12   John Helton, *The insufficiency of the light of nature: exemplified in the vices and depravity of the heathen world* (London: printed for John and Arthur Arch, and John Wright, 1797), 82–83.

John Helton was an itinerant preacher with John Wesley, later a Quaker.

authority. This test is an impossible test to pass for all except one man—Jesus.

Through this test, all humanity would be required to recognize its sin. It is inescapable. This test would form two groups of people: those who recognize their sin as revealed through God's yardstick of righteousness and those who refuse to recognize God's authority to dictate right and wrong. It is so profoundly elegant and simple how God uses something seemingly unsophisticated like ten rules to define a population. This test is an impetus for rebellion or contrition. Every person takes this test.

In daily operations in the US Army, we have volumes of regulations that no one person could possibly know. God has just ten regulations and even reduces their essence to two. "'Teacher, which is the greatest commandment in the Law?' Jesus replied: 'Love the Lord your God with all your heart and with all your soul and with all your mind. This is the first and greatest commandment. And the second is like it: Love your neighbor as yourself. All the Law and the Prophets hang on these two commandments'" (Matthew 22:36–40).

Lamentations 3:40–42 says, "Let us examine our ways and test them, and let us return to the Lord. Let us lift up our hearts and our hands to God in heaven, and say: 'We have sinned and rebelled and you have not forgiven.'"

Jeremiah sought renewal for his people, his nation of Israel. This renewal would start through the people, ending their rebellion. They would then examine themselves as compared to the Lord and his righteousness. Jeremiah wanted to restore the community using the criteria of God's righteousness. God's righteousness, not any human version of righteousness, is our baseline of success. God uses his Word to communicate his standard of holiness to us. His words are plain and readily available. God advertises this benchmark well in Scripture.

There is one catch, though. You have to lend your heart and ear. You have to demonstrate an element of desire. Even a smidge will get you started. God can provide this to you; just ask! Jeremiah 6:16, Matthew

13:10–17, Mark 6:4–6, and Acts 28:23–28 show this, as do the following verses.

> Then I heard the voice of the Lord saying, "Whom shall I send? And who will go for us?" And I said, "Here am I. Send me!" He said, "Go and tell this people: 'Be ever hearing, but never understanding; be ever seeing, but never perceiving.'" (Isaiah 6:8–9)

> Since they did not know the righteousness that comes from God and sought to establish their own (their own version of righteousness), they did not submit to God's righteousness … But not all the Israelites accepted the good news. For Isaiah says, "Lord, who has believed our message?" Consequently, faith comes from hearing the message, and the message is heard through the word of Christ. But I ask: Did they not hear? Of course they did: "Their voice has gone out into all the earth, their words to the ends of the world." (Romans 10:3, 16–18)

Some failed this test—likely most. The people would not believe the Word of God or even God's Son. Jesus told them this much: it does not matter if the Word is written, read, or even spoken. If they did not believe the Word, then his witness and physical appearing were worthless to them. This test reveals if you believe or disbelieve God's Word.

Zechariah 13:8–9 (NKJV) says, "'And it shall come to pass in all the land,' Says the Lord, 'That two-thirds in it shall be cut off and die, But one-third shall be left in it: I will bring the one-third through the fire, Will refine them as silver is refined, And test them as gold is tested. They will call on My name, And I will answer them. I will say, "This is My people"; And each one will say, "The Lord is my God."'"[13] Through this test, God introduced adversity. Through this adversity, the people would call on God. This test restored a legacy of identity and purpose, thus perpetuating their shared history.

---

13   Jack W. Hayford, Ed., *New Spirit Filled Life Bible*, New King James Version (Nashville: Thomas Nelson Inc., 2002), 1262.

In Acts 5:1-10, Ananias and Sapphira sold a piece of property. They claimed to donate all the proceeds to the church. They actually donated a smaller portion. They kept back some for themselves, claiming to have donated 100 percent of the sale. "Peter said to her, 'How could you agree to test the Spirit of the Lord? Look! The feet of the men who buried your husband are at the door, and they will carry you out also'" (Acts 5:9).

Ananias and Sapphira tested the Spirit of the Lord. They failed corporately. They also failed separate tests with respect to their responsibility not to lie. As a result, great fear and respect of God's holiness fell on the church. The entire group was very much affected. This test reminded the entire group, the church, that sin and orchestrating a lie are serious affronts to the Spirit of the Lord.

The Word of God is sufficient evidence for belief. Apollos preached that Jesus was the Messiah in public debate. He used the Scriptures to prove what he preached. He tested the instruction he had received from Pricilla and Aquila and found that it was accurate within the Scriptures. Apollos armed himself with the proven truth to preach about Jesus Christ to advance God's kingdom. The Pharisees challenged Jesus about his witness in the book of John. John 8:13 says, "Here you are, appearing as your own witness; your testimony is not valid." The religious leaders quipped to Jesus. Jesus stated in John 3:17-18, "In your own Law it is written that the testimony of two men is valid. I am one who testifies for myself; my other witness is the Father, who sent me."

In John 5:31-47, Jesus delivered the same tough message. Jesus told the religious leaders that the reason they did not believe he was God's Son was that they did not love God. They showed no effort to seek the praise that came from God. They refused to believe the prophets, because the Word did not dwell in them, and they never believed the Word of God from the beginning. In John 5:47, Jesus responded to the pious leadership: "But since you do not believe what he (Moses) wrote, how are you going to believe what I say?"

From these two illustrations, we know that Scripture can be tested and found true. In fact, we are obliged to confirm this truth for ourselves. Apollos and Jesus both testified to this fact. We will go into this proof test a few more times in this book. Chapter 3 will strengthen this position further.

First Timothy 3 identifies the criteria churches can use to choose deacons. These criteria are still in use in some denominations to segregate the greater church population in order to select their deacons. The church needs spiritually mature men for this leadership position, and this criterion facilitates their selection based on Biblical instruction. This test defines the purpose and the criteria for membership into this group.

First Timothy 5:19 establishes a way to test accusers. Elders, a governing body, may be required to make unpopular decisions. To protect elders, accusations are to be tested. Those seeking retribution with untruths are more likely to be screened out. This test protects the integrity and viability of the body of elders.

First John 4:1–6 says,

> Dear friends, do not believe every spirit, but test the spirits to see whether they are from God, because many false prophets have gone out into the world. This is how you can recognize the Spirit of God: Every spirit that acknowledges Jesus Christ has come in the flesh is from God, but every spirit that does not acknowledge Jesus is not from God. This is the spirit of the antichrist, which you have heard is coming and even now is already in the world. You, dear children, are from God and have overcome them, because the one who is in you is greater than the one who is in the world. They are from the world and therefore speak from the viewpoint of the world, and the world listens to them. We are from God, and whoever knows God listens to us; but whoever is not from God does not listen to us. This is how we recognize the Spirit of truth and the spirit of falsehood.

The Bible is full of stories, parables, and vignettes. This is a way the Bible's message can transcend time so well. First John 4:1–6 is one of the very few step-for-step examples in the Bible. These criteria give us systematic instructions on how to know if a person speaks from the truth of God. This will let us know where allegiances fall.

All of these tests have a common denominator: they derive their foundation in the truth of God's character. God's character is the source of Jesus' authority in the Ephesus model. The center of gravity in each of the nine Biblical examples is identical—a set of common core values. We use these same core values to define our group we call the church.

God defines the core values of the church through his criteria of holiness and righteousness. These common core values apply to everyone in the church. This commonality builds our community of purpose with meaning, the foundation of our hope. There is a reciprocating climate of mutual respect from the church to the individual. The church must maintain a disciplined purpose and message that does not drift from established core values—God's values. The church experiences success through God's provision, protection, and salvation. This is hope realized. Hope is the point that first brought us to the church. The church perseveres in unity with a legacy of shared history.

These stages build into a community with members who have a sense of belonging. The past message and purpose are the same message and purpose at present. Scripture uses the root word *persevere* (Revelation 2:2-3) twice in the Ephesus text. Legacy is in perseverance. "I the Lord do not change" (Malachi 3:6). "Jesus Christ is the same yesterday and today and forever" (Hebrews 13:8).

The Reward of Ephesus

Romans 12:2-5 is a good bridge from this lesson of Ephesus—testing. It demonstrates how shared values of a community culminate in the reward that is a sense of belonging.

> Do not conform any longer to the pattern of this world, but be transformed by the renewing of your mind. Then you will be able to test and approve what God's will is—his good, pleasing

and perfect will. For by the grace given me I say to every one of you: Do not think of yourself more highly than you ought, but rather think of yourself with sober judgment, in accordance with the measure of faith God has given you. Just as each of us has one body with many members, and these members do not all have the same function, so in Christ we who are many form one body, and *each member belongs to all the others.* (Emphasis added.)

Through the test of belief in Jesus Christ as our Savior, we will receive the reward of Ephesus: our sense of belonging. We will belong to God! He is eternal, and we will receive eternal life through his goodness to us.

A sense of belonging is the foundational and the most important reward we take from the seven churches. Look at the reward identified in Revelation 2:7 (NKJV): "He who has an ear, let him hear what the Spirit says to the churches. To him who overcomes I will give to eat from the tree of life, which is in the midst of the Paradise of God."[14]

From the book of Genesis, we know that access to the Tree of Life was restricted to prevent us from being permanently stuck in this present fallen sinful condition (Genesis 3:22). So we also know from Revelation 2:7 that we will not always be stuck in our fallen state. It is God's plan to restore our relationship to him and allow us to live forever in his care and his domain. We who belong to Christ have an eternal future inside the community of God and his holy righteousness. Our sense of belonging is from God and to God.

We also know that people individually matter to God. Our invitation is to the midst of the paradise of God. Our invitation is not to some austere outpost. God does not deposit or relegate us to some inconsequential station in life on the periphery of relevance in which we are told to try not to break anything. We are in the middle of God's existence. We are accepted and acceptable in his venue. God desires restoration of our relationship with him. We matter to him.

---

14   Jack W. Hayford, Ed., *New Spirit Filled Life Bible,* New King James Version (Nashville: Thomas Nelson Inc., 2002), 1819.

We are relevant, because God ascribes us relevance. Only God has the authority to grant a sense of belonging to him.

We have a sense of belonging to and from God. The attraction is reciprocal as long as we do not rebel and dismiss God and his laws from our lives. Secular scholarship also recognizes the importance of an in-kind or reciprocal relationship between the individual and the group.

One may ask, *So how do I know if I truly belong to God? What is this whole sense of belonging to and from God, anyway?* We each have the same test to pass. We know the criterion of the test is God's holiness. So we know this test is a valid test. That is essential. It is construct number one in the Ephesus model. Take the test right now.

> Everyone who believes that Jesus is the Christ is born of God, and everyone who loves the father loves his child as well. This is how we know that we love the children of God: by loving God and carrying out his commands. This is love for God: to obey his commands. And his commands are not burdensome, for everyone born of God overcomes the world. This is the victory that has overcome the world, even our faith. Who is it that overcomes the world? Only he who believes that Jesus is the Son of God. (1 John 5:1–5)

In Jesus, we have a sense of belonging, because he is the agent of first cause and the source that defines the church. He is the giver of the criteria that define the church's identity and a subsequent sense of belonging. This is the most important concept. We will build upon this foundation—the entire framework for scriptural leadership.

If this foundation cracks, our minds will find no rest, and relationships, organizations, and societies will break down. If you travel to any other city in life before traveling to Ephesus, you will never know how to structure your life. You will have no foundational sense of belonging. Your starting points will be plural, arbitrary, and nebulous; chaos will follow. "For this reason I kneel before the Father, from whom his whole family in heaven and on earth derives its name" (Ephesians 3:14–15).

CHAPTER 2

The Churches: Smyrna

See, he is puffed up; his desires are not upright-
but the righteous will live by his faith.

—Habakkuk 2:4

Welcome to Smyrna

This is where giants of the faith live, for now. These pillars of the faith definitely belong to God, so we will need to check our pride before entering through the gates of this city. We will do well to use two eyes, two ears, and only one mouth while we are here.

We also have two concepts to learn in this city. They are under the headings *Contrite* and *Life*. The lesson is being contrite or humble, and the reward is life. Let us meet the people in the second church!

Revelation 2:8-11 was written to the church in Smyrna:

> To the angel of the church in Smyrna write: These are the words of him who is the First and the Last, who died and came to life again. I know your afflictions and your poverty-yet you are rich! I know the slander of those who say they are Jews and are not, but are a synagogue of Satan. Do not be afraid of what you are about to suffer. I tell you, the devil will put some of you in prison to test you, and you will suffer persecution

for ten days. Be faithful, even to the point of death, and I will give you the crown of life. He who has an ear, let him hear what the Spirit says to the churches. He who overcomes will not be hurt at all by the second death.

Outline

The Stages of the Ephesus Model—Sense of Belonging

Stage 1: The lesson is the test, and the reward is a sense of belonging.

Stage 2: The lesson is humility, and the reward is life.

Stage 3: The lesson is to know the Word and know your job, and the rewards are individual worth and value.

Stage 4: The lesson is to have a heart, and the reward is individual responsibility to support the group.

Stage 5: The lesson is to keep focus, and the rewards are rest, companions, protection, and contentment.

Stage 6: The lesson is enablement, and the reward is credibility.

Stage 7: The lesson is not to forget, and the reward is autonomy to lead and create.

Sense of Belonging—Stage Two

Smyrna is the second city. That means we will use the second construct in the Ephesus model to help us understand and interpret the Scripture dealing with this church. In stage two of the Ephesus model, potential members must recognize the criteria and their giver as legitimate and coherent in order to define a discrete entity of purpose. The group must have a common set of core values that will apply to all the members. These are the foundations of their hope.

One of the core concepts of a sense of belonging is that we must recognize the foundational authority as legitimate, and the group, in turn, must value the individual. There must be a reciprocal relationship of in-kind respect. The organization must recognize the individual as a good fit. The individual must also recognize the organization as a good fit for him or her. The street runs both ways. This respect is essential in a viable organization, functional family, or healthy church. Apart from mutual respect, members have no reason to maintain a presence inside the domain of an organization.

In this stage of a sense of belonging (Ephesus model), the individual recognizes the authority of an agent of first cause to establish criteria to define a group. This is an evaluation for the individual, since a determination is made if the group and its authority are legitimate or not. The individual has already been deemed to be a good fit from the group's perspective. The ball is in the individual's court now.

The individual scrutinizes the organization. Upon entry, the person will be associated with that group's identity. This is an important decision that an individual will not take lightly. Reputations are at stake with potential embarrassment if things go badly.

This is why in Revelation 2:8, the Lord identifies himself with such majesty and power. This is a dazzling display of power and ultimate authority. As the first and the last, he transcends time and dimensions. He died and came back to life, demonstrating absolute existential sovereignty. He has the power of life. He advertises himself as legitimate. He shows himself to be a safe bet with potential members.

He is a worthy authority and a sovereign agent of first cause; therefore, his organization, the church, is legitimate. His holiness and righteousness define the core values and criteria that in turn define the entity, the church. Potential members must choose Jesus and his holiness and righteousness to gain entrance. The church of Smyrna chose Jesus.

The Smyrna church receives only commendation from Jesus. There is an air of mutual respect communicated in Revelation 2:9–10. Jesus respected this church in Smyrna. There can be no doubt this church had a grounded sense of belonging to God.

Like Smyrna, we also need to know that it is possible for us to achieve our own respect from God (John 5:44). We need to know we are part of the purpose of the church and can contribute with meaning. We must know our decision to follow Jesus will not be for naught. This is the hope that causes private individuals to become members of the church. Outside of hope in a purpose, why would any organization exist?

But how did this church get to the level of mutual respect? Its people were humble and contrite.

The Lesson

Thinking back to our previous lesson of testing, we will also see that the church community in Smyrna experienced a test. This church received no criticism from Jesus. Its members even thrived under the pressure of the test. There were many martyrs for Christ's sake in this church's age.

Even Polycarp, the bishop of this church, was put to death for his Christian beliefs. During the Smyrna age, people had to publically affirm, "Caesar is Lord," and for that affirmation receive some form of a certificate from the government validating their loyalty. Polycarp refused to renounce Christ and was martyred on February 23, AD 155. Polycarp, before his death, said, "Eighty and six years have I served him and he has done me no wrong. How can I blaspheme my King who saved me?"[15]

There were persecutions of Christians under ten Roman emperors. This is the symbolic meaning of "ten days" in Revelation 2:10. Christians were the objects of blood sport in Roman sporting events. Men of unbelief in power killed, boiled, burned, crucified, and used Christians as prey for wild animals for spectacle.[16] All of this evil was committed under the orchestration of the Devil and his minions to

---

15   John P. Newport, *The Lion and the Lamb: A Commentary On The Book Of Revelation For Today* (Nashville: Broadman Press, 1986), 146.

16   Timothy Lahaye, *Revelation Unveiled* (Grand Rapids: Zondervan, 1999), 52.

destroy the church. Since you are reading this book, I presume it to be a safe assumption the Devil was not successful.

This church is under tribulation and persecution, and its people demonstrated a spirit of poverty. This is a contrite community of believers in Christ Jesus. Look at some biblical examples of those who demonstrated contriteness or humility. Before we move on, we need to understand the most correct use of the word *poverty*.

Revelation 2:9 uses the word *poverty*. The Bible does not say the people of Smyrna were in economic straits. Their poverty was an acknowledgement of their spiritual humility. This is a description of their attitude. To be poor in spirit is another way to say this. They relinquished a dominating spirit based in self-pride for a contrite spirit of reliance on God. They surrendered their condition to the Lord and his ways, even when they were subjected to martyrdom. Poverty in this context describes their attitudes, not their bank accounts.[17]

Being humble and contrite will set the tenor for our stay here in Smyrna. Our attitude is a big deal in this city.

The spirit of contriteness reveals another truth—the truth of God's gentle hand as he develops our relationship to him. One of the overarching purposes of the seven churches collectively reveals how Christ gets to know his bride—the church.[18] Just as a man would not propose on the first date, God allows us room to get to know him.

The Lord uses an ancient method as a model in his courtship. Genesis outlines this "get to know you first" model. It is the God-Lord God-Lord demonstration. In Genesis 1, the Creator went by the name of God. There was a very businesslike decorum in the Scripture as he created. God did not seem approachable. In fact, he seemed aloof and distant. From Chapters 2–3, God went by the name of Lord God. One might even think he was warming up to humanity. In Chapter 4,

---

17   Barbara Frale, *The Templars: A Secret History Revealed* (New York: Arcade, 2009), 27–28.

18   Roger P. Elwood, Comp., *The Second Coming, Billy Sunday, Great Sermons Volume One* (Uhrichsville: Barbour Publishing, 1998), 320.

Eve called him "Lord." This is the very first instance in which he is referred to as Lord in Scripture.

In the tomb after his resurrection, Jesus first revealed himself to a woman also. In John 20:10–18, Mary Magdalene cried, since the body of her *Lord* was not in the tomb. Then she recognized Jesus. The Lord is most involved in our lives when we are most in need. Our attitude toward the Lord will attract or repel us to him. Our attitudes are an offering or an offense to God.

Notice the difference between Adam and Eve in Genesis 3. Some scholars reason Adam committed the very first sin. It was a sin of omission. Eve's second sin was a sin of commission. When God confronted Adam about his sin, he became defiant. Eve was contrite. It is no wonder the Lord revealed himself as Lord, a caring provider, to Eve first (Genesis 4:1). This is when she became pregnant. Eve's contrite attitude unlocked the true character of God, allowing her to perceive God as a caring Lord. Eve met God where he was, and the Lord met Eve where she was.

Defiance and Humility

The differences of attitude between David and Saul separated them, eliciting opposite responses from God. In 1 Samuel 15:30, Saul replied, "I have sinned. But please honor me before the elders of my people and before Israel; come back with me, so that I may worship the Lord your God." In this verse, Saul was not contrite or remorseful of his self-acknowledged sin. He only wished to be elevated once again in the sight of the elders and people by Samuel, the prophet. He did not even acknowledge God as his own. Saul had no sense of belonging to God, which was shown when he said to the prophet, Samuel, "the Lord *your* God."

Saul was in the process of losing his sense of acceptance from the people of his nation and therefore his sense of belonging. Saul's situation deteriorated rapidly. Chaos nipped at his heels. Remember from our first lesson and first reward that a sense of belonging from and to God is a driver of order, structure, and coherence. A lack of a sense of belonging generates the opposite—chaos. Chaos is the natural inverse of a sense of belonging from and to God. Saul trended toward chaos.

Look at another king to see how he reacted to his own sin. King David took full ownership of his sin in 2 Samuel 12:13. "Then David said to Nathan, 'I have sinned against the Lord.' Nathan replied, 'The Lord has taken away your sin. You are not going to die.'"

David rightly said, "I have sinned against the Lord." King Saul only wanted Samuel to get him out of the doghouse, as it were. Saul was only sorry that he was caught. David demonstrated a contrite spirit with a guilty-as-charged attitude. This is an attitude God can work with. We can shun God with our free will if we choose that. That attitude says to God, *I am in charge, I can handle anything that happens in my life, and you are not welcome here.*

The Synagogue Ruler

In Mark 5:22–24, Jairus, a synagogue ruler, pleaded earnestly at Jesus' feet for the life of his sick daughter. This would have been a huge step of public faith and humility for Jairus, since the religious leadership was almost categorically opposed to Jesus. Jairus would not win many friends or impress his leadership by acknowledging Jesus' power. Jairus recognized Jesus as legitimate and placed his hope in him (stage two of the Ephesus model).

Other Examples of Humility

- Numbers 12:3: "Now Moses was a very humble man, more humble than anyone else on the face of the earth."

- First Kings 21:20, 29: King Ahab humbles himself before God and Elijah—"Because he has humbled himself, I will not bring this disaster in his day."

- Second Chronicles 7:11–14: "If my people, who are called by my name, will humble themselves ..."

- Micah 6:8: "What does the Lord require of you? To act justly and to love mercy and to walk humbly with your God."

- Habakkuk 2:4: "See, he is puffed up; his desires are not upright."

- Matthew 5:1-12: The Beatitudes

- Matthew 8:5-13: The faith of the Centurion—"Lord I do not deserve to have you come under my roof. But just say the word ..."

- Matthew 15:22-28: The faith of the Canaanite woman—she asked for mercy.

- Mark 1:40-42: A man with leprosy was healed—"and begged him (Jesus) on his knees ..."

- Mark 7:31-35: The healing of a deaf and mute man—"and they begged him (Jesus) to place his hand on the man."

- Mark 9:14-29: The healing of a boy with an evil spirit—"take pity on us and help us."

- Mark 10:46-52: Blind Bartimaeus received his sight—"Jesus, Son of David, have mercy on me!"

- Luke 7:11-17: Jesus raised a widow's son—"When the Lord saw her, his heart went out to her and he said, 'Don't cry.'"

- James 4:6-10: "God opposes the proud but gives grace to the humble. ... Humble yourselves before the Lord, and he will lift you up."

Humility and being contrite toward God and his authority will lead us to a place of mutual respect with God. We do not need to be godlike to attain respect from God. We only need to be what he created us to be. In fact, the desire to be godlike is specifically prohibited by God in Genesis 2-3. This is the sin of rebellion, as we try to define our own versions of what we say is right and what we say is wrong.[19] This sin embodies the fall and spawns all subsequent sins. Pride is a God repellant. Humility is like perfume to God.

The people in the church of Smyrna wore the perfume of a contrite spirit. They attained mutual respect from God. God promised to give them the crown of life and to keep them from the second death (Revelation 2:10–11). He offers life! A contrite attitude points the way to this reward.

The Reward of Smyrna

Revelation 2:10–11 says, "Be faithful, even to the point of death, and I will give you the crown of life. He who has an ear, let him hear what the Spirit says to the churches. He who overcomes will not be hurt at all by the second death." *These verses are about life and death.* They are also about the giving of the gift of life through the ability to live. This is the most profound and simple of the lessons of the churches. We have life.

We have life, and we also depend on God to sustain our lives. He sustains them through provisions. Psalm 56:13 says, "For you have delivered me from death and my feet from stumbling, that I may walk before God in the light of life."

D .L. Moody (1837–1899) preached a sermon called "Mary and Martha":

> Do you remember that Elijah got under that juniper tree and laid down and wished himself dead? There was God's representative on earth, the man that stood nearer to the throne of God than any man on the face of the earth at that time, wishing himself dead! An angel came and woke him up, and said, "Rise and eat," and there was a cake there on the coals and a cruse of water, and he got refreshed. After he got refreshed, he fell asleep again. I presume he hadn't had

---

19   Ravi Zacharias, *In the Course of Human Events*, Ravi Zacharias International Ministries, 2010, compact disc.

39

any sleep for days and nights; perhaps hadn't had any food; he was so full of zeal. The zeal of the Lord was just eating him right up. He had another sleep, and the angel woke him up again and said, "Rise and eat," and he rose, and there was a cake that had been cooked, and a cruse of water. The Lord didn't upbraid him then; the Lord didn't test him then. He fed him and got him rested, and then when He got him off into Horeb, He said, "Elijah, what doest thou here?" Then God took him in hand and dealt with him; *but He fed him first and got him rested.*[20] (Emphasis added.)

We are physical beings, and God knows we need all the things that sustain our bodies. In 2 Timothy 4:13, the apostle Paul spoke to Timothy: "When you come, bring the cloak that I left with Carpus at Troas, and my scrolls, especially the parchments."

Paul asked for three items: his cloak, scrolls, and parchments. During this detention, Paul needed his friend, Timothy, to bring three items to support his needs—specifically, his physical need (cloak), his mind (scrolls), and his spirit (parchments).[21] The very first thing Paul asked for was his ability to sustain his physical body. It is true Paul said, "especially the parchments," but he did not mention them first.

We have life in the context of the one to whom we belong—God. God is able to give us life and sustain our lives. He is the Creator (Genesis 1:1). We must be contrite to acknowledge this, because with that acknowledgement, we submit ourselves willingly to God's authority, laws, and favor. Through acknowledgement of Genesis 1:1, God offers us a sense of belonging.

If you derive your core sense of belonging from anything except the God of the lesson of Ephesus, you do not exist inside the domain of any authority capable to provide life. Life comes from God alone.

20   Roger P. Elwood, Comp., *Mary and Martha*, D. L. Moody, *Great Sermons Volume One* (Uhrichsville: Barbour Publishing, 1998), 168–169.

21   Gregory N. Barkman, "Addressing Physical Needs," September 23, 2011, MP3 file, downloaded June 24, 2013, http://www.sermonaudio.com/semoninfo.asp?SID=92411842393.

No other entity has a stake in this domain, and life is independently relevant and valuable. When we view life as being derived from God, life becomes its own reference point. Smyrna has passed her lesson of humility, and the reward is life.

God will take care of those who belong to him (James 4:10). When we receive our belonging from God, we are God's own children. The Devil is not quite as generous or caring for his children. David teaches us through Psalm 37:25, "I was young and now I am old, yet I have never seen the righteous forsaken or their children begging bread."

This reward of Smyrna is life and the ability to sustain our physical beings. This is the second of seven rewards in God's method of order. In A. H. Maslow's hierarchy of needs, physiological needs are the most basic needs. This is Maslow's foundational need, roughly shown as his first of five. "A person who is lacking food, safety, love, and esteem would most probably hunger for food more strongly than for anything else."[22]

Maslow likely would not recognize a sense of belonging to or from God as a valid need and may categorize this need as myth or imagined need. Maslow's hierarchy and this method of order start in nearly the same place. I say nearly the same place, because I characterize the reward of Smyrna as life. It is life and the ability to sustain life. This is the second reward in the method of order. Maslow recognizes our physiological needs or the ability to sustain life as the foundational need. Nevertheless, he never quite elevates life itself to its rightful sacred status.

Without a sense of belonging from God, the Creator and progenitor of all life, how could anyone know to recognize life as sacred? Furthermore, has any science ever explained the essence of life? How can the unbeliever explain consciousness emerging from the inanimate?

---

22   A. H. Maslow, "A Theory of Human Motivation," *Classics in the History of Psychology,* posted August 2000, http://psychclassics.yorku.ca/Maslow/ motivation.htm.

For the believer, it does not require much intellectual horsepower to answer the question *Where does life come from?* This question is the obvious companion question to, "Mama, where do babies come from?" Life is the breathing elephant in the unbeliever's living room.

Maslow makes a clear and conscious departure from Scripture.[23] I was somewhat comforted by this, only because this demonstrates that Maslow must have known Scripture to argue against Scripture. Maslow writes, "Freedom, love, community feeling, respect, philosophy, may all be waved aside as fripperies which are useless since they fail to fill the stomach. Such a man may fairly be said to live by bread alone."[24]

This reference is an allusion to the temptation of Jesus in the book of Matthew by the Devil in the wilderness. Jesus defended himself with Scripture from the book of Deuteronomy: "Man does not live by bread alone but on every word that comes from the mouth of God" (Deuteronomy 8:3 and Matthew 4:4). We must be humble to accept our subordinate role to God. We must give God his rightful glory and respect God's Word and life with the rightful, regal status they deserve.

Humility can be a tough lesson. It is essential that we acknowledge the purpose of Revelation 2:8, when Jesus displayed his power in such a majestic way. He wants you to join with him. That was the intent of the dazzling display of power—to show us he is holy and righteous with all sovereign power. He even has the power of life (Revelation 2:10–11). We can place our hope in him. This is a central theme in stage

---

23   I do not claim to know Maslow's religious views, if any. I introduce Maslow for two reasons. First, I borrow his idea to construct a tiered hierarchy, only one entirely based in Scripture. Second, his allusion to Scripture may mean we start our thinking for this aspect in the same place, even if we come to different conclusions. It should also be noted that another hierarchy is recorded in 2 Peter 1:5–8.

24   A. H. Maslow, "A Theory of Human Motivation," *Classics in the History of Psychology*, posted August 2000, http://psychclassics.yorku.ca/Maslow/motivation.htm.

two of the Ephesus model. You must humble yourself to align yourself with his criteria defined by his holiness.

We will use this lesson in all of the cities we travel to, but we will use it the most in our next city of Pergamum. The teachers of Pergamum are already expecting us in their school. The lesson plans are ancient and very relevant. We will do some more thinking in our next destination. Are you ready to learn? Do not worry about academic acceptance letters. Ephesus has already forwarded the transcripts that verify our sense of belonging from God. Everything is ready for our arrival!

CHAPTER 3

The Churches: Pergamum

Now all has been heard; here is the conclusion of the matter: Fear God and keep his commandments, for this is the whole duty of man.

—Ecclesiastes 12:13

Welcome to Pergamum

In 1999–2000, I was in OCS (Officer Candidate School), where leadership skills are developed, sometimes through unconventional methods. The candidates all take their turn being the platoon leader (PL) and platoon sergeant (PSG), a few iterations throughout the course of the school. The instructors, especially in the first days, will fire off instructions to the PL at such a rate that it will be impossible to keep track of the changes in venue, uniform, training event, etc. It is only a matter of time before the officer candidates become spilt up with some in the right place and some not, some in the right uniforms and some not, some with the correct equipment and some not.

This is the instructor's opportunity to dress down an individual candidate for not following instructions with not-so-subtle implications of trying to sabotage the team. Then, as if on cue, the candidate will respond by saying, "I did not get the word." Bingo. That was the exact word-for-word response the instructors were looking for (or not looking for). The sharks smelled blood as they circled. "Oh? You didn't get the word? Is that right, candidate? Well in that case, let me get you the word!"

Then this unfortunate soul would be provided a twenty-five-pound rock with a wire cage wrapped around it with a lopped-off stick for a handle. It was painted blue with white lettering—*the word*. This soldier would carry this burden as a sign to all involved. The principal point is that you do not blame other people for your mistakes. That is a very unbecoming action and a slippery slope of blame-deflecting that will destroy a team. We have *individual responsibilities* to support the team; this was learned in a fundamental way.

Pergamum has good schools, and you should expect to train hard and learn valuable skills here. There is a lesson and a reward in this city also. They are under the headings *the Word* and *Individual Worth*.

Jeremiah 6:16 will be a recurring theme in this book. It outlines a formula or model for individual cognition and learning. This model will foster our ability to fulfill our individual responsibilities that we all have in learning. Jeremiah 6:16 says, "This is what the Lord says: 'Stand at the crossroads and look; ask for the ancient paths, ask where the good way is, and walk in it, and you will find rest for your souls.'" Jeremiah 6:16, interpreted from the student's perspective, says, *stop, learn, do, rest*.

Personal responsibility is a large part of our learning in Pergamum. We have personal responsibility to God's Word and personal responsibility in daily affairs. The schools in Pergamum will facilitate these lessons. The schools here are good with serious lessons. Let us meet the people in the third church!

Revelation 2:12–17 was written to the church in Pergamum:

> To the angel of the church in Pergamum write: These are the words of him who has the sharp, double-edged sword. I know where you live–where Satan has his throne. Yet you remain true to my name. You did not renounce your faith in me, even in the days of Antipas, my faithful witness, who was put to death in your city–where Satan lives. Nevertheless, I have a

few things against you: You have people there who hold to the teaching of Balaam, who taught Balak to entice the Israelites to sin by eating food sacrificed to idols and by committing sexual immorality. Likewise you also have those who hold to the teaching of the Nicolaitans. Repent therefore! Otherwise, I will soon come to you and will fight against them with the sword of my mouth. He who has an ear, let him hear what the Spirit says to the churches. To him who overcomes, I will give some of the hidden manna. I will also give him a white stone with a new name written on it, known only to him who receives it.

Outline

The Stages of the Ephesus Model—Sense of Belonging

Stage 1: The lesson is the test, and the reward is a sense of belonging.

Stage 2: The lesson is humility, and the reward is life.

Stage 3: The lesson is to know the Word and know your job, and the rewards are individual worth and value.

Stage 4: The lesson is to have a heart, and the reward is individual responsibility to support the group.

Stage 5: The lesson is to keep focus, and the rewards are rest, companions, protection, and contentment.

Stage 6: The lesson is enablement, and the reward is credibility.

Stage 7: The lesson is not to forget, and the reward is autonomy to lead and create.

Sense of Belonging—Stage Three

Pergamum is the third city. That means we will use the third construct in the Ephesus model to help us understand and interpret the Scripture dealing with this church. Stage three of the Ephesus model states that you must have members. They must collectively operate inside the predetermined scope of purpose identified at the start by the giver through defining criteria. The members must be loyal to the group and its founder or founding authority. The group must struggle through adversity—a problem or threat—to solidify the bond. This brings the group to life with spirit of personality.

In this stage, the potential members have become full members in the organization. They are now stakeholders. They recognize the organization as credible, because the criteria that define the organization's purpose are legitimate. The agent of first cause is also viewed as legitimate. However, without any struggle, meaningful bonds will not form, and the organization's identity will not be expressed. Adversity will establish these bonds, and their spirit of personality will well up from within the organization. Then people outside the group will be able to peg the group's identity.

In Revelation 2:13, we can see that this church had members who were stakeholders and were true and faithful. This church faced an external threat from a false religion. Remember, the people of Ephesus had an internal problem of forgetting their first love or the object of that love—God. This third stage will highlight the need for a group to strive through external difficulties and emerge intact. This church must emerge with the same identity it started with. The churches' meaning and purpose are contingent upon this identity. Continuity will retain the spirit of personality.

We need adversity to create and strengthen lateral and vertical bonds that are the sinews of any group. The church will need strong individual members in this stage. The Lord mentioned Antipas by name for this reason. The martyr Antipas lived this example of strength for the churches to see. We also see that some did not do so well with this external threat in Revelation 2:14–15.

Satan had influence in this city, and he was the external threat acting against the church. Jesus did not send the church out empty-handed against Satan. He equipped them with what they needed to survive in a high-threat environment. He provided them with the sword of the Word to live in a rough neighborhood (Revelation 2:12–13).

Jesus reminded them (and us) that we need the Word and his Spirit. Through his Word, his Spirit will join to our spirits. The Word and our responsibility to seek and know the Word is a central lesson in this city of Pergamum. His Word is our defense in our own high-threat environments.

The Lesson

We have individual tasks and responsibilities in life. We must live up to our end of the bargain. Only an individual can accomplish individual responsibilities. I had a baseball coach who used to stress to us, the players, that he wanted only four things from us—that we should be able to run, catch, throw, and hit. That was it.

Of course, those are just isolated components of the game. It is a whole other thing to incorporate those four aspects in a coherent way to fulfill obligations to the team as an individual player. The individual must be competent, and it takes individual effort to be competent.

Antipas was mentioned by name for all the right reasons. It is no coincidence the Scripture mentions Anitpas, an individual, by name during stage three of our Ephesus model. This reference to Antipas teaches us a key lesson. Members must meet their individual obligations to support the church or any organization. This is true for our employment as well.

Our central lesson for Pergamum is that we have an individual duty to know Scripture. We also have an individual duty to know our jobs well and be competent. Other people will count on us. It is our job not to let them down.

Martin Luther was a champion of the divine importance of our tasks or occupations, no matter how small or great people may view them to be.[25] Daily work is God's work, as Martin Luther would correctly characterize it. Comprehension of Scripture in an emaciated state is not possible. Therefore, the farm tractor mechanic must support God's work as much as the professional pastor. After all, from where did the mechanic receive his gift in the first place?

The Word as a Weapon

Jesus wasted no time in telling the church of Pergamum about the sword. This reference is the first item on the agenda. It is first, because it is important.

This text uses the word *sword* twice (Revelation 2:12, 16). The sword is associated with Jesus' mouth or in speaking. The sword represents the *Word*. These are three examples in Scripture that help us understand what the word *sword* represents.

1. Isaiah 49:2: "He made my mouth like a sharpened sword, in the shadow of his hand he hid me; he made me into a polished arrow and concealed me in his quiver."

2. Ephesians 6:10–18 speaks of the armor of God, and Ephesians 6:17 says, "Take the helmet of salvation and the sword of the Spirit, which is the word of God."

3. Hebrews 4:12: "For the word of God is living and active. Sharper than any double-edged sword."

In Ephesians 6:17, notice that the *Word* is the only offensive weapon in the armor of God. This is the offensive weapon Pergamum needed. What is the Word? You might be surprised.

Psalm 138:1–2 says, "I will praise you, O Lord, with all my heart; before the 'gods' I will sing your praise. I will bow down toward your holy temple and will praise your name for your love and your faithfulness, for you have exalted above all things your name and your word." John 1:1–5 says, "In the beginning was the Word, and the

25   Timothy Keller and Katherine Leary Alsdorf, *Every Good Endeavor: Connecting Your Work to God's Work* (New York: Dutton, 2012), 69-73.

Word was with God, and the Word was God. He was with God in the beginning. Through him all things were made; without him nothing was made that has been made. In him was life, and that life was the light of men. The light shines in the darkness, but the darkness has not understood it."

George Whitefield (1714–1770), the famous eighteenth-century English preacher during the Great Awakening, outlines some points for the individual to know for studying Scripture. I have edited these points from his sermon, "The Duty of Searching the Scriptures."[26] "Scriptures were written, even to show us the way of salvation, by Jesus Christ ... search the Scriptures with a humble childlike disposition. A desire to do the will of God is the only way to know it ... make an application of everything you read to your own hearts. Christ's words are spirit, and they are life only understood through the Spirit. Ask the Spirit to guide you into all truth."

The Word is Scripture, and the Word is Jesus. It is a mystery. As George Whitefield taught, the words of Christ are spirit.

Jesus showed the church in Pergamum that the Word has use as protection. He told this church that rough days were ahead, and he equipped them for survival. Jesus outfits us with Scripture in the same way. Jesus has already set this precedent. Look at the Word in action as a sword of defense.

In Matthew 4:1–11, the temptation of Jesus, Jesus responded to the Devil with Scripture in order to formulate a defense.

- It is written: man does not live by bread alone, but on every word that comes from the mouth of God.

- It is also written: do not put the Lord your God to the test.

- It is written: worship the Lord your God, and serve him only.

---

26   Roger P. Elwood, Comp., *The Duty of Searching the Scriptures, George Whitfield, Great Sermons Volume One* (Uhrichsville: Barbour Publishing, 1998), 142–146.

Jesus defended himself and actively opposed the Devil with Scripture. In Matthew 4:4, Deuteronomy 8:3 was the origin of this rebuttal. The ability to quote from Deuteronomy by heart speaks volumes. Sure, he is Jesus, but I am still impressed. The takeaway is that the Word has power, and it takes individual work to get it inside head and heart. It is a big task.

We Require Adversity

The church in Pergamum was in a rough neighborhood. Jesus knew that. This adversity was part of this church's development. This gave its members an opportunity to mature under adversity and a chance to prove themselves faithful (Revelation 2:13). Proving faith is possible neither when times are good nor when life is easy.

Apart from tough times, how would we ever know the true character of our organizations or of ourselves? I have had three combat tours. I know that dark days can bring out the best in people and an organization. Dark days can even justify the existence of the organization and individual roles in that organization.

These dark days establish meaningful lifelong bonds laterally and meaningful vertical bonds with the greater entity. The identity of the individual is fully linked to the identity of the organization because of these dark days. Adversity causes us to grow and develop. Just as driving a nail in a fruit tree will encourage it to bear fruit, adversity in our lives will also bring about fruit. Adversity is like a train; a train that rolls on parallel tracks of personal development and maturity until we arrive at the destination called Meaning. Purpose meets us on the platform.

McMillan and Chavis express the same ideas that the ancient lesson of Pergamum portrays from ages past. "Personal investment is an important contributor to a person's feeling of group membership and to his or her sense of community. McMillan (1976) contended (a) that working for membership will provide a feeling that one has earned a place in the group and (b) that, as a consequence of this personal investment, membership will be more meaningful and valuable."[27]

So you may ask, What good is the Scripture? Why would I place any faith in it or seek out Scripture as a guide for my life? What value is it to me when I am in adversity? These are valid points that we all must answer. Below is an answer with depth and meaning. This is significant, because if the Scripture proves to be true, our obligation to follow it is inescapable.

Sid Roth is a Messianic Jew and host of the TV show *Sid Roth's It's Supernatural!* In his book *They Thought for Themselves,* he captures the Old Testament prophesies and their relevance to Jesus in an interesting way.

In the Scriptures, God gives over 300 prophesies that clearly identify the Messiah. According to the law of compound probabilities, there is only one chance in 33,554,432 that even 25 of these prophecies could be fulfilled by a single person.

Whoever has fulfilled the following prophecies is the true Messiah of Israel. The Messiah would

- be born in Bethlehem of Judah (see Micah 5:1–2).

- be born of a virgin as a miracle sign to the Jewish people (see Isa. 7:14). The Hebrew word for virgin used in Isaiah 7:14 is *almah*. This is translated in some versions of the Bible as "maiden" or "young woman." However, in the Jewish Scriptures, when *almah* is used and read in context, it is almost always clear that it refers to "a virgin." Furthermore, God promised Israel "a sign." It would not be a sign for a normal young maiden to bear a child. It *would* be a sign if a *virgin* gave birth to a

---

27   David W. McMillan and David M. Chavis, "Sense of Community: A Definition and Theory," *Journal of Community Psychology* Vol. 14 (January 1986): 10.

McMillian 1976 refers to an unpublished manuscript of David W. McMillan at George Peabody College for Teachers, Nashville, Tennessee, in the bibliography of "Sense of Community: A Definition and Theory," *Journal of Community Psychology* Vol. 14 (January 1986).

child by the hand of God. Please note that the Hebrew name of this Child, *Immanuel*, means, "God with us." This shows His unusual nature. Some stumble at this prophecy because of their lack of faith. God, who put the universe in place, could have easily had a virgin bear a child. Besides, what is that compared to God's marvelous creation of a human being!

- be despised and rejected of men (see Isa. 53:3).

- live a sinless life (see Isa. 53:9).

- be betrayed for 30 pieces of silver (see Zech. 11:12–13).

- die for the sins of the Jewish people and the whole world (see Isa. 53:5–6, 8).

- die by crucifixion (see Ps. 22:14–18; Zech. 12:10).

- have his clothing gambled for at the time of His death (see Ps. 22:18).

- come before the destruction of the Second Temple (A.D. 70) (see Daniel 9:24–26).

- arise from the dead (see Ps. 16:10; 110:1).

Only *one man* in history has fulfilled these prophecies. He has changed the calendar and the course of history; and millions of Jews and Gentiles have trusted Him for their personal atonement. His Hebrew name is Yeshua, which means, "salvation." To my non-Jewish friends He is known as "Jesus," which was originally translated from the Greek as Je'sus (hay-SOOS) Christos (CHRIS-tose), and was later anglicized as "Jesus, The Christ," which means, "Salvation, The Messiah"![28]

Even still many will not believe the Word of God. I cannot help but wonder with which fulfilled prophesy unbelievers take exception. Which fulfilled prophesy proves God is a make-believe myth and

---

28   Sid Roth, *They Thought For Themselves: Ten amazing Jews* (Shippensburg: Destiny Image, 2009), 221–223.

Jesus is a poser? Even secular scholars and Muslims believe Jesus actually existed as a person, perhaps as a prophet or teacher. The question remains: is Jesus a charlatan?

If the Word was God and Jesus is the Word, as demonstrated in John 1, then the companion question is, is the word truth? Again, which fulfilled prophesy would you take issue with if you are an unbeliever? Each prophesy is an open invitation to disprove Scripture. Each prediction is a potential liability—a very deep hole—yet each fulfillment becomes a well of credibility.

If the Word of God is true, we are on the hook to seek, know, and do what Scripture says. We must confront this individual responsibility on our own. We must decide. We are obligated to support our organizations and employers with faithful sincerity as well. We must be faithful, even in adversity. Our very identity links to these points. These points will lead us to the reward of Pergamum.

The Reward of Pergamum

Revelation 2:17 says, "He who has an ear, let him hear what the Spirit says to the churches. To him who overcomes, I will give some hidden manna. I will also give him a white stone with a new name written on it, known only to him who receives it." The overcomer will receive three things according to this verse. They are manna, a white stone, and a new name. These three items have symbolic meaning. The overcomer will receive provision, acquittal, and identity. Said another way, he or she will receive liberty and purpose.

Let us look at the manna. Of course, this is the sustenance provision for the children of Israel in the wilderness of the Sinai as Moses (Exodus 16) led them to the Promised Land. No one knows what manna is, but we do know it was a divinely provided food for the Israelites when food was scarce and starvation seemed to be a real possibility. Our ability to live—even life itself—comes in the form of provision of necessities for our physical being, such as air, food, water, shelter, clothing, etc. We know from this verse that the Lord cares for and about our physical needs.

A white stone is what an ancient jury would use to cast a "not guilty" vote.[29] It is an acquittal from our confessed sins through Christ; it is liberty. We know from this verse that the judgment rendered is in our favor from the highest court. We could not have pulled that off unless Jesus Christ was our advocate. God gives us divine authority to live and operate in the physical and intellectual contexts of our families, organizations, and nation. After all, God made us in his own image. He has those qualities, and we have those same qualities.

On the white stone was a new and secret name. This is a license for us to be who we are, and we are all different. Each stone is unique. Therefore, each one of us is unique. Individuals have inherent special worth in and of themselves inside God's structure.

The three aspects outlined in this text are provision, liberty, and identity. These three components combined and said in a succinct, fused way is this: *You have unique intrinsic value as an individual.*

When God cast each of us, he broke the mold afterward. You do not acquire, gain, or lose value based upon performance or net worth. Your value as a unique individual (reward of Pergamum) is a reference point in and of itself when viewed in the context that the life you are given (reward of Smyrna), which has been imparted to you from God, to whom you belong (reward of Ephesus). This is God's method. It is his order.

It is time to travel to the next city, but before we say our goodbyes in Pergamum, do not forget that you will need to remember what you learned in this Pergamum school. Do not worry; since you have traveled to all the cities in order, learned your lessons, and gained their associated rewards, you are fully qualified and educated to perform your duty in Thyatira. The people of Thyatira are not lazy, so look alive, and perk up.

---

29 *The Quest Study Bible,* New International Version (Grand Rapids: Zondervan Publishing House, 1994), 1712.

Jack W. Hayford, Ed., *New Spirit Filled Life Bible,* New King James Version (Nashville: Thomas Nelson Inc., 2002), 1820.

Chapter 4

The Churches: Thyatira

As iron sharpens iron, so one man sharpens another.

—Proverbs 27:17

Welcome to Thyatira

In USMC boot camp, we had our boots, low quarter black shoes, running shoes, and shower shoes all lined up in a hierarchy under our bunks. The recruit on the top bunk had his lineup on the inside; the recruit on the lower bunk had his lineup on the outside, all in an orderly way. Well, of course, someone will invariably get the system wrong or not keep all the toes lined up, or something else will disturb this apparently extremely critical aspect of barracks keeping.

An infraction of this requirement makes it plainly clear to the drill instructors (DIs) that the recruits have no desire to seek uniformity or develop teamwork. The recruits, obviously, are willfully defying the DIs' simple instructions. So the DIs will help us achieve uniformity and teamwork. The DIs, while the recruits are not in the barracks, will put every boot in sight in a pile. Now they are all uniform.

If there are eighty recruits in the platoon, then this pile will consist of 160 boots, hopefully. Now the recruits—in order to foster teamwork, which is clearly deficient—will be provided a generous two minutes to find their boots. Make no mistake; you will find *your boots*. These boots may be two left feet or a size twelve and a size nine, but you will get two boots and move out. Once we got a little time within the next couple of days, we unraveled the boot mess. Mostly everyone got the correct boots back—or at least boots they could live with. I have to hand it to the DIs; we did work together as a team to get our boot issue unraveled. We took a better interest in supporting the team after that. If we saw a buddy's boot-shoe hierarchy in trouble, we helped him out.

We have a lesson and a reward to glean from this city as well. The lesson and reward are under the headings *Choosing a Heart* and *Corporate Responsibility*. Think of Thyatira as an industrial town whose people work together, you will need your lesson from Pergamum handy, so do not forget what you have learned. Are you ready to join in the work? Let us meet the people in the fourth church!

Revelation 2:18-29 was written to the church in Thyatira:

> To the angel of the church in Thyatira write: These are the words of the Son of God, whose eyes are like blazing fire and whose feet are like burnished bronze. I know your deeds, your love and faith, your service and perseverance, and that you are now doing more than you did at first. Nevertheless, I have this against you: You tolerate that woman Jezebel, who calls herself a prophetess. By her teaching she misleads my servants into sexual immorality and the eating of food sacrificed to idols. I have given her time to repent of her immorality, but she is unwilling. So I will cast her on a bed of suffering, and I will make those who commit adultery with her suffer intensely, unless they repent of her ways. I will strike her children dead. Then all the churches will know that I am he who searches hearts and minds, and I will repay each of you according to your deeds. Now I say to the rest of you in Thyatira, to you who do not hold to her teaching and have not learned Satan's so-called deep secrets (I will not impose any other burden on you): Only hold on to what you have until I come. To him who overcomes and does my will to the end, I will give authority over the nations—"He will rule them with an iron scepter, he

will dash them to pieces like pottery"—just as I have received authority from my Father. I will also give him the morning star. He who has an ear, let him hear what the Spirit says to the churches.

Outline

The Stages of the Ephesus Model—Sense of Belonging

Stage 1: The lesson is the test, and the reward is a sense of belonging.

Stage 2: The lesson is humility, and the reward is life.

Stage 3: The lesson is to know the Word and know your job, and the rewards are individual worth and value.

Stage 4: The lesson is to have a heart, and the reward is individual responsibility to support the group.

Stage 5: The lesson is to keep focus, and the rewards are rest, companions, protection, and contentment.

Stage 6: The lesson is enablement, and the reward is credibility.

Stage 7: The lesson is not to forget, and the reward is autonomy to lead and create.

Sense of Belonging—Stage Four

Thyatira is the fourth city. That means we will use the fourth construct in the Ephesus Model to help us understand and interpret the Scripture dealing with this church. Stage four of the Ephesus model states that the group must value its individual members.

A mob shares stages one through three with a healthy organization. A mob and a single individual have mutual affinity and a job to do, even if it is nefarious. However, a mob places no value on the single individual. Organizations do. People are the lifeblood of any organization, and the organization must respect this fact. The military perspective is that an army is not made of rifles, trucks, and tanks; those items are equipment. Armies are people. People count, especially the people who are least able to fend for themselves.

Alligators eat their own young. Organizations cannot. Organizations are people, and each person matters.

In Ephesus, Jesus walked among the lampstands to evaluate the churches, his newly formed organization (Revelations 2:1). In Thyatira, Jesus did a similar task. He searched the hearts and minds of the individual members (Revelation 2:23). Jesus told us he has eyes like blazing fire and feet like burnished bronze (Revelation 2:18). Meaning Jesus is present and scanning throughout the church. This tells us he is physically with all the churches and watches all the churches (Revelation 2:18-19, 23).

As Jesus watched, he evaluated the church. Jesus is specifically evaluating our deeds of love, faith, and service toward other people.

We know from stage four of a sense of belonging in the Ephesus model that individuals matter to the group. The church of Thyatira valued her people. They did well at deeds of love, faith, service, and perseverance. Jesus commended this church for placing value on the individual (Revelation 2:19). Sardis would be told to remember what Thyatira taught it (Revelation 3:3), further proving that Thyatira was on track in this respect.

Not every member in this church was on track, though. Some members chose to follow Jezebel. She was an internal threat to the church. She was involved with idolatry, adultery, and sexual immorality. This conduct did not place value on the individual. This conduct was better suited for a mob. The members had to choose between Jesus and Jezebel. The onus was on them.

The Lesson

Thyatira received praise from Jesus for deeds of love, faith, service, and perseverance. What does this mean? Jesus commended them for having a heart for the people they served and led. We also must have a heart of love for those we serve and lead. People matter, most especially the people we are beholden to lead and support. This applies to the church and our daily work equally. This is a conscious decision.

In Revelation 2:21, we see that Jezebel was unwilling to repent of her sin. Ignorance was not a factor in this case; it was an outright refusal to repent. Humility precedes repentance. We covered that lesson in Smyrna with having a contrite and humble attitude. The problem is that people like Jezebel reject repentance. The onus is on us—the people—in the same way.

The lesson of Thyatira is that we must lead with a heart. We must show our love for those whom we lead. We have to choose to do this. This is a sacred responsibility. A common idiom states, "I do not care how much you know before I know how much you care."

Choosing God's Heart

Even after Jesus had done all these miraculous signs in their presence, they still would not believe in him. This was to fulfill the word of Isaiah the prophet: "Lord, who has believed our message and to whom has the arm of the Lord been revealed?" For this reason they could not believe, because, as Isaiah says elsewhere: "He has blinded their eyes and deadened their hearts, so they can neither see with their eyes, nor understand with their hearts, nor turn—and I would heal them." (John 12:37-40)

In John 12, we see that the people *would* not believe, which caused an attitude where they *could* not believe. Their unbelief affected their own hearts. Even though Jesus worked miracles in their very presence, they still would not believe. This happens every day.

Heaven is full of volunteers, not conscripts. Hell, likewise, is full of volunteers, not conscripts. Remember that the church is the bride of Christ.[30] This is not an arranged marriage (Revelation 19:7). The Lord will receive anyone who loves him. We are all predestined to salvation, but some freely, consciously, and deliberately choose Satan (Ephesians 1, Mark 3:29). We are not hollow puppets acting out a play. We all choose our Lord, be that a holy one or a profane one. Just as Eve and Mary Magdalene chose their Lord (Chapter 2), we must choose in the same way.

You do not invite yourself to other people's houses, and in the same way, you do not invite yourself to God's heaven. Heaven is God's domain, not ours, so we are obligated to follow God's rules of entry, not our own rules. We are guests in his domain.

Why would you want to go to God's heaven anyway if you are not a believer? The joy of heaven is fellowship with God. Heaven is merely a venue; it is not the main point here. If you desire to be with God for eternity, Jesus can settle this issue. Jesus is at the door of salvation; he controls entrance into God's heaven (Revelation 3:20).

God will not force you to love him or even seek him and his heart of love. That is exactly how we are, too. Do you want a friend who you have to coerce to love you? What joy is in that? Are we not made in God's own image? That is a distasteful idea to us. Apparently, it is a distasteful idea to God.

Below is Scripture that proves the Lord reveals himself worthy, and we, in turn, must choose his righteousness. The onus is on us. There is no one to deflect our own blame or fault when we will not seek the Lord. When we refuse to know his Word, we actually deny God's authority to author his Word. How insulted would you be if you were God? Ironically, in our postmodern world, print and knowledge abound with disproportionate unbelief.

This seeking and knowing is a general and larger point—that is to say, one of the fundamental intents of the Bible. Here are a few examples in which God showed us his heart of love for his people.

---

30   Roger P. Elwood, Comp., *The Second Coming, Billy Sunday, Great Sermons Volume One* (Uhrichsville: Barbour Publishing, 1998), 320.

People matter to an organization, and in the same way, we matter to God.

1. Genesis 4:6-7: "Then the Lord said to Cain, 'Why are you angry? Why is your face downcast? If you do what is right, will you not be accepted? But if you do not do what is right, sin is crouching at your door; it desires to have you, but you must master it.'"

2. Exodus 19:4-6: "You yourselves have seen what I did to Egypt, and how I carried you on eagle's wings and brought you to myself. Now if you obey me fully and keep my covenant, then out of all nations you will be my treasured possession. Although the whole earth is mine, you will be for me a kingdom of priests and a holy nation (Israel)."

3. Second Chronicles 31:20-21: "This is what (King) Hezekiah did throughout Judah, doing what was good and right and faithful before the Lord his God. In everything that he undertook in the service of God's temple and in obedience to the law and the commands, he sought his God and worked wholeheartedly. And so he prospered."

4. Psalm 27:4: "One thing I ask of the Lord, this is what I seek: that I may dwell in the house of the Lord all the days of my life, to gaze upon the beauty of the Lord and to seek him in his temple."

5. Jeremiah 3:14: "'Return, faithless people,' declares the Lord, 'for I am your husband, I will choose you—one from a town and two from a clan—and bring you to Zion.'"

6. Joel 3:14: "Multitudes, multitudes in the valley of decision! For the day of the Lord is near in the valley of decision."

7. Matthew 7:7-8: "Ask and it will be given to you; seek and you will find; knock and the door will be opened to you. For everyone who asks receives; he who seeks finds; and to him who knocks, the door will be opened."

8. Matthew 18:10–14 (the parable of the lost sheep): "See that you do not look down on one of these little ones. For I tell you that their angels in heaven always see the face of my Father in heaven. What do you think? If a man owns a hundred sheep, and one of them wanders away, will he not leave the ninety-nine on the hills and go to look for the one that wandered off? And if he finds it, I tell you the truth, he is happier about that one sheep than about the ninety-nine that did not wander off. In the same way your Father in heaven is not willing that any of these little ones should be lost."

9. Matthew 23:37: "O Jerusalem, Jerusalem, you who kill the prophets and stone those sent to you, how often I have longed to gather your children together, as a hen gathers her chicks under her wings, but you were not willing."

10. John 3:16: "For God so loved the world that he gave his one and only Son, that whoever believes in him shall not perish but have eternal life."

11. John 10:14–18: "I am the good shepherd; I know my sheep and my sheep know me—just as the Father knows me and I know the Father—and I lay down my life for the sheep. I have other sheep (Gentiles) that are not of this sheep pen. I must bring them also. They too will listen to my voice, and there shall be one flock and one shepherd. The reason my Father loves me is that I lay down my life–only to take it up again. No one takes it from me, but I lay it down of my own accord. I have authority to lay it down and authority to take it up again. This command I receive from my Father."

12. First John 4:7–21 shows God's love. First John 4:9: "This is how God showed his love among us: He sent his one and only Son into the world that we might live through him."

13. Genesis 1:1: "In the beginning God created the heavens and the earth."

God revealed his heart when he created heaven and invited us to be with him in heaven. God never wanted anyone to go to hell. Note that in the beginning, God created only the heavens and the earth (Genesis 1:1). Watchman Nee says it like this: "Why do some people not have any spiritual ear? Because (1) they have no spiritual aspiration, and (2) they are in fact afraid of the Lord's word (Matthew 13:13-15)."[31]

It has always been this way. Abraham had to choose God. He had to choose to obey God. The Israelites had to choose God (Exodus 19:7-8, 24:3, 7; Deuteronomy 26:17-19, Psalms 26:4-5, 105). We have to choose God.

Israel Zangwill (1864-1926) had the idea of the Jews being the choosing chosen. Rabbi Gilbert S. Rosenthal says, "Israel Zangwill put it aptly: 'It is not so much a matter of the chosen people as the choosing people.' There is a dialectic to it all; a process of reciprocity is at work."[32]

God presented himself worthy to Abraham, and Abraham chose God; God chose Abraham back. It is requited love God desires, as shown in Jeremiah 3:11-15. God is the first cause (stage one of the Ephesus model), but the exchange is still a mystery. God presents himself worthy to us the same way. This is our opportunity to exercise our onus to choose him and lead with the same heart of love (stage two of the Ephesus model).

You do not have to be a biblical scholar to know Jesus preached to the masses. What does that tell us? His message is not meant for any specific demographic or the elite; it is for everyone. Jesus showed his own heart of love to all the people. It is an open-ended offer—a call to worship and believe. We know from Smyrna that a contrite attitude is

31   Watchman Nee, *Come, Lord Jesus* (New York: Christian Fellowship Publishers. Inc., 1976), 23.

32   Gilbert S. Rosenthal, "Some Are Chosen, All Are Loved," Boston College, accessed January 30, 2013, http://www.bc.edu/dam/files/research_sites/cjl/texts/cjrelations/resources/articles/rosenthal.htm.
See *Chosen Peoples* by Israel Zangwill.

the key that unlocks our ability to see God for who he is. He is always the same.

We must lead the same way Jesus leads us. Jesus is not brutal like Stalin. He does not operate killing fields like Pol Pot. He does not crush lives like Chairman Mao. He does not burn children, handicapped people, and Jews in ovens. Jesus was crucified on the cross as a sacrifice for all of our sins. He offered himself and his blood as a living sacrifice (Leviticus 17:11) so that we could have eternal life with him in heaven. This is his heart. Each person has to choose whether that is the heart he or she wants also.

No person has exemption. We all will eventually choose. When we choose Jesus and his heart of love, he will give us the reward of Thyatira.

The Reward of Thyatira

When I was in Ranger School in Fort Benning, Georgia, I had to lead the platoon and receive a grade on my performance each time I was in charge. In one instance after I completed my term, some Green Berets who were in my platoon from the special forces community pulled me to the side discreetly and offered me some advice. They suggested that I consider leading this way or that way in the future when a certain situation came up again. They floated some options for me to consider in tactical situations that were sure to be useful in future operations.

These guys were true professionals, and if anyone had it together, they did. They were going to pass Ranger School; this point was not in too much doubt, apart from being hit by a random meteorite or something like that. They could have just closed up, concerned themselves with getting through Ranger School, and let the others fend for themselves. They did not do that. These guys showed their hearts. They were the exact opposite of "Hey, everybody, look over here and see how great I am," even though that would have actually been founded. I listened to their leadership and took their tactical advice.

Revelation 2:26–29 is about being in a position of authority and using that authority in a responsible way. Supporting the group with authority is the reward.

From General Eisenhower's 1948 book, *Crusade in Europe:*

> General Marshall gave long and earnest attention to the selection of individuals to occupy key spots in overseas commands and in the reorganized department. In the process he sometimes gave clear indication of the types of men who in his opinion were unsuited for high position. Foremost among these was the one who seemed self-seeking in the matter of promotion.[33]

This reward of authority comes with a price tag, though. Authority without character will generate a climate of angst in an organization. In Pergamum, we had a job, and that job was to develop ourselves to be able and just leaders by the time we get to Thyatira. Just leadership is a function of character.

We cannot skip around from lesson to lesson. Order matters; we have to learn each stage and lesson systematically. Each lesson, each city, and each church builds upon the others, and their cumulative rewards will structure our lives. This is how God develops us so we will not become liabilities to our own societies. As God leads, we learn to lead. God's order is coherent.

If leaders are promoted before they are ready, everyone will suffer—the leader and the led. The leader's self-esteem will suffer; he or she will be rattled. The leader may not fully recover personally or professionally. We are responsible to the group, and we owe our subordinates leadership founded in true character. This is a sacred responsibility.

This is not about personal gain. This is about the servant-leader. People count on us to lead justly. God places leaders in authority,

---

33   Dwight D. Eisenhower, *Crusade in Europe* (New York: Doubleday and Company, Inc., 1948), 50–51.

and we must not betray that gift (Hebrews 13:17). This is the reward Thyatira.

This is the most difficult lesson. If you arrive in Thyatira with an inadequate or short-circuited education from Pergamum, you will never reach your potential, and subordinates will suffer because of your incompetence or character issues. However, if you are an able and just leader, you will have fulfillment in that your purpose is relevant and meaningful, and the collective will benefit because of you.

Pack up to prepare for the next city. Sardis is not a resort town. We have some work to do, but you will be very glad to know you will get some much-needed rest there. Between the testing of Ephesus, humbling ourselves in Smyrna, learning hard lessons in Pergamum schools, and contributing to the team without prodding in Thyatira, you are probably worn out by now. Thyatira holds the hardest lesson, so you can breathe a little easier from here on out. We are well over halfway now, so stay on track. This is the downhill stretch.

CHAPTER 5

The Churches: Sardis

Bloom where you're planted. Pray, "Lord,
help my heart to sit down."[34]

—Chuck Norris

Welcome to Sardis

When conducting patrols in the infantry, you must plan the route. Every person in the patrol must know the route for obvious reasons. Direction and distance to each checkpoint along the way are written down in a code or memorized so the planned route cannot be compromised by the enemy. The route should not be drawn on the map in case those who intend us harm recover it. During the patrol, the leader will periodically signal to the compass man to confirm his azimuth. After walking over rough terrain, cutting through thick brush, or crossing a creek, it is easy to get pointed in the wrong direction. The leader knows this. Therefore, the leader periodically checks and crosschecks the azimuth to ensure he leads the patrol in the right direction. This is the leader's assurance that they will hit the predetermined checkpoint. The leader must stay on track.

---

34   Chuck Norris, *The Official Chuck Norris Fact Book: 101 of Chuck's Favorite Facts and Stories* (Carol Stream: Tyndale House Publishers, Inc., 2009), 61.

We also have two concepts to learn in this city. They are under the headings *Focus* and *Contentment*. The lesson is maintaining focus, and the reward is contentment. Let us go meet the people in the fifth church!

Revelation 3:1–6 was written to the church in Sardis:

> To the angel of the church in Sardis write: These are the words of him who holds the seven spirits of God and the seven stars. I know your deeds; you have a reputation of being alive, but you are dead. Wake up! Strengthen what remains and is about to die, for I have not found your deeds complete in the sight of my God. Remember, therefore, what you have received and heard; obey it, and repent, But if you do not wake up, I will come like a thief, and you will not know at what time I will come to you. Yet you have a few people in Sardis who have not soiled their clothes. They will walk with me, dressed in white, for they are worthy. He who overcomes will, like them, be dressed in white. I will never blot out his name from the book of life, but will acknowledge his name before my Father and his angels. He who has an ear, let him hear what the Spirit says to the churches.

Outline

The Stages of the Ephesus Model—Sense of Belonging

Stage 1: The lesson is the test, and the reward is a sense of belonging.

Stage 2: The lesson is humility, and the reward is life.

Stage 3: The lesson is to know the Word and know your job, and the rewards are individual worth and value.

Stage 4: The lesson is to have a heart, and the reward is individual responsibility to support the group.

Stage 5: The lesson is to keep focus, and the rewards are rest, companions, protection, and contentment.

Stage 6: The lesson is enablement, and the reward is credibility.

Stage 7: The lesson is not to forget, and the reward is autonomy to lead and create.

Sense of Belonging—Stage Five

Sardis is the fifth city. That means we will use the fifth construct in the Ephesus model to help us understand and interpret the Scripture dealing with this church. Stage five of the Ephesus model states that the agent of first cause with authority and empowered members must retain discretion to make corrective actions so the group will stay on message and mission. This will retain the charter identity of the group.

We have done some heavy lifting thus far in our other cities, so you will be glad to know we will get some rest here, although not right away. In Pergamum, we went to school and had to do some hard individual work to prepare ourselves to arrive in Thyatira fully equipped and mature. In Thyatira, we were responsible to support the group as competent individuals and as just leaders. Both of these tasks were difficult and required dedication. They were very labor-intensive. Here in Sardis, we will be able to slow down to catch our breath and dial back the intensity. However, before we relax, we will have to learn about our focus. We must keep focus and remain true to our organization's charter intent.

Right away in Revelation 3:1, Jesus reminds us he holds the seven stars. He told us that in our very first city, Ephesus. Why would he tell us this information again? We need to hear it again. Sardis needs an azimuth check. Its people are off track. The church has walked over rough terrain, and its people got pointed in the wrong direction.

Jesus told them that they were not what they seemed. Jesus even told them to remember what they received and heard and then obey it (Revelation 3:3). What did they receive and hear?

From our discussion in this book's Introduction, we know we can view the churches in a number of different ways. We will continue to use this historical chronological view (Newport 1986) to answer the question "What did they receive?" from verse 3. That means we will look at the previous city and church we visited in Thyatira.

Revelation 2:19 states that the church of Sardis received instruction in love, faith, service, and perseverance from the church of Thyatira. Sardis received its heart from the hard-working church of Thyatira. However, Sardis was mostly off track. Some members were still on track, though (Revelation 3:4).

This was an internal threat from within this church. This fifth stage of sense of belonging will direct us to our lesson for Sardis. The lesson is to keep focus.

The Lesson

You cannot navigate life with a cookbook of solutions. Every situation is different, and we will need to gauge, with our hearts, all the seemingly infinite number of variables associated with each problem as we interact with our families, peers, and those for whom we work. Life is way too complex for any list of do's and don'ts.

This baseline of truth is how and why the Bible is applicable in every time, situation, and culture. Sure, the Bible has some ground floor boundaries like the Ten Commandments, but it is also a guidebook for an infinite number of applications. The Bible is perpetually relevant.

One of the baseline points that does not go away is commitment. We must be faithful in every aspect of our lives. Jesus told the Sardis church this also. Wake up! (Revelation 3:2, 3) Snap out of it! Get back to work. Get back on track. There will be time for rest later, but not right now.

The central lesson in Sardis is to keep focus. This will lead us to the reward. The reward of Sardis is rest, companionship, protection, and contentment. Rest is good, but it must be at the right time.

The Reward of Sardis

A good transition from getting back on track and finding rest and contentment in Jesus is in Matthew 11:28–30: "Come to me, all you who are weary and burdened, and I will give you rest. Take my yoke upon you and learn from me, for I am gentle and humble in heart, and you will find rest for your souls. For my yoke is easy and my burden is light."

We will diagram these verses with respect to our lessons and rewards thus far in our journey. You will see that we are definitely on to something valuable and on the right track with what I teach. This one excerpt captures the essence of the first five churches of Ephesus, Smyrna, Pergamum, Thyatira, and Sardis.

- "Come to me … take my yoke"—that is a sense of belonging. We received this in Ephesus. Working together with Jesus is also the lesson of Thyatira, the industrious town, where we contributed to the team's goals.

- "I am gentle and humble." Being contrite and humble is our lesson from Smyrna.

- "I am gentle and humble in heart, and you will find rest for your soul." Jesus told the people of Sardis to remember their hearts—the hearts that Thyatira gave them. Rest is a reward of Sardis.

- "Take my yoke upon you and learn from me." We went to school in Pergamum and had to work hard so that we could learn God's righteousness and prepare ourselves to be future competent team members.

- "For my yoke is easy and my burden is light." This is rest, protection, and contentment—the reward of Sardis.

Revelation 3:4–6 reveals the reward that we will receive in Sardis. We touched on it in Matthew 11:28–30 above, but we will go into more detail here.

In Sardis, we walk with the Lord; we do not even have a destination (Revelation 3:4). We are just walking. We are dressed alike, too. We are his companion and friend, and we spend time together just for the sake of spending time together. We are able to be close to the Lord, because he has made us worthy, and while we are close, we can get to know each other.

We are in God's protection in Sardis. What harmful thing could get us when we walk with the Lord? The Lord controls our salvation, and our names will remain in the Book of Life. Sardis is a nonthreatening destination. We have room and license to exist and grow here; we can be normal here. Our personality types dictate normal for each of us. We have contentment here. We have shown others our hearts, and God shows us his humble heart.

Companionship is a seldom-mentioned aspect of God's character that belies its importance. We are able to have companionship with God and other people. Because God is good to us, he allows us to be his friends. He has also structured our existence so that we can have mutual friends among our peers.

We know that companionship is part of God's plan, because it is part of being made in the likeness of God (Genesis 1:26, 9:6). God is three in one, and he is not alone within himself. He has community and companionship within himself. He is the Father, Son, and Holy Spirit. He has always been this way. We learn this during the creation story and other places in the Bible also. A few supporting Scriptures are Genesis 1:26, 3:22, 6:3; Isaiah 6:8; Matthew 28:19; John 1:1–3, 14:26, 15:15; 1 John 5:7–8; and Jude 20–21.

This is a good place to arrive, but you had to go through some tough lessons in other cities to get here with your rewards. In Ephesus, God calls us to contrition to recognize his holy authority. This is how we belong to God. We continued in our humility in Smyrna, gaining provision for this life and our eternal life from the Lord Jesus Christ. The schools in Pergamum were tough, and we had to pull our weight. We contributed our work to support the collective team in Thyatira. In Sardis, we finally got a chance to rest in our contentment in a protected environment. Sardis is not our final destination. This is just a much-needed respite to catch our breath.

We all need a place where we can let our guard down—a place where we know others seek our best interest. This is evident and manifest through physical protection, ideological affiliations, cultural approval, and religious bonds. These religious bonds are the ties of God's Word in which we, our church, and our greater community of Christians trust and believe.

When I return home from a combat theater, one of the aspects I have to adjust to is not having sentries on watch and not having radio traffic white noise in the background. In theater, we publish a perpetual guard roster and a patrol tracker. Someone is always on duty for the purpose of security. Additionally, there is always radio traffic crackling in the Tactical Operations Center (TOC). You always have an ear lent to that traffic, and it becomes a part of you, like a heartbeat.

The normal, steady state traffic on the network is very settling, since through this tone, you know your sector is quiet when you are not physically in sector yourself. You continuously and subconsciously listen to the radio for that out-of-place twinge. You listen for that small inflection in a soldier's voice, from slight duress to a full-blown TIC (troops in contact) event. Your entire consciousness is devoted to opposing a threat.

The fact that someone is always awake and on duty for the purpose of protection and running current operations is very comforting and settling to your entire being. Then, all of a sudden, when you redeploy, are at home, and go to bed at night, no one is awake. There is no guard roster, and no radio traffic is crackling from security patrols outside the wire or sentries inside the wire. There is no smell of gun oil, diesel smoke, shift change bustle, or helicopter noise, and everything is entirely too quiet—suspiciously quiet. It is decidedly unsettling at first. The comfort noise and troop movements are gone. Your community of purpose is disbanded or in transformation. Your individual role is in a paradigm shift. The center of gravity of your sense of belonging is in transition. Your renewed civilian life can seem very pedestrian compared to combat operations.

Now the consciousness that was an asset can be a liability. You have to deliberately flip the home switch and reintegrate into a new, tame, normal society.

That takes some getting used to. Everything that communicated safety, protection, and contentment to you is now gone. You have to find a completely new normal. The normal you knew in theater is no more, and the normal you knew prior to your deployment to theater is absent as well. This is all new territory. This adjustment requires flexibility.

Reintegration has proven to be tough business for the military. More suicides by far occur during this critical phase. We have to take heart. Rest and contentment in Christ can trump the disheveled life changes and unsettling adjustments associated with redeployments and other significant life events as well. Contentment is achievable; Sardis teaches us this much.

The next two cities will be a little different from these last five. Therefore, we will consolidate what we have learned thus far before we leave for Philadelphia.

Table 1

Ephesus	God is holy; that is the criterion for our test of belief. We accept his offer, choosing to belong to him and worship him, since we know that we are far from holy.
Smyrna	With a contrite attitude, we submit to God's authority in our lives. Our hope is in Jesus. He sustains our lives throughout eternity.
Pergamum	We study God's Word to develop ourselves. We continue to learn and grow in competence and acumen in preparation for our next assignments.
Thyatira	We must use our gifts and skills we developed as subordinates inside the group. This will prepare us to be leaders of the group when we are ready and capable to lead.
Sardis	Stay on track, and keep focus; keep working. In Jesus, we will have rest, companionship, protection, and contentment.

I know we are all content here, but do not let that lull you into staying in Sardis too long. We have only two more churches to visit, and we are rested enough, so let us travel to the next city. Do not worry. You will like it.

CHAPTER 6

The Churches: Philadelphia

The capacity of soldiers for absorbing punishment and
enduring privations is almost inexhaustible so long as
they believe they are getting a square deal, that their
commanders are looking out for them, and that their own
accomplishments are understood and appreciated.[35]

—General Eisenhower

Welcome to Philadelphia

This is a great city—the best city you have visited so far. If you have
made your way here along the mail route and not skipped around, I
know you belong to God (reward of Ephesus). He looks out for your
life on earth and your eternal life as well (reward of Smyrna). You are
an important and valuable person individually (reward of Pergamum).
You contributed to the team in a unique way that only you could
provide (reward of Thyatira). You are content (reward of Sardis). You
might think, *That seems like everything, all aspects are covered. What could
be next?* In this church, we will receive recognition—well, only the
recognition we rightfully deserve. You will see.

---

35   Dwight D. Eisenhower, *Crusade in Europe* (New York: Doubleday and
Company, Inc., 1948), 354.

Before we start, remember our second city, Smyrna. In the land of spiritual giants, we were careful to tread lightly out of respect for the martyrs. This allowed us to learn better from those Christians there. We were careful in Smyrna to use two eyes, two ears, and only one mouth. Philadelphia has spiritual giants, too, so we will want to be very attentive and respectful in this city also.

We also have two concepts to learn in this city. They are under the headings *Enablement* and *Credibility*. The lesson is being enabled, and the reward is credibility. Let us get moving and go meet the people in the sixth church!

Revelation 3:7-13 was written to the church in Philadelphia:

> To the angel of the church in Philadelphia write: These are the words of him who is holy and true, who holds the key of David. What he opens no one can shut, and what he shuts no one can open. I know your deeds. See, I have placed before you an open door that no one can shut. I know that you have little strength, yet you have kept my word and have not denied my name. I will make those who are of the synagogue of Satan, who claim to be Jews though they are not, but are liars-I will make them come and fall down at your feet and acknowledge that I have loved you. Since you have kept my commandment to endure patiently, I will also keep you from the hour of trial that is going to come upon the whole world to test those who live on the earth. I am coming soon. Hold on to what you have, so that no one will take your crown. Him who overcomes I will make a pillar in the temple of my God. Never again will he leave it. I will write on him the name of my God and the name of the city of my God; the new Jerusalem, which is coming down out of heaven from my God; and I will also write on him my new name. He who has an ear, let him hear what the Spirit says to the churches.

Outline

The Stages of the Ephesus Model—Sense of Belonging

Stage 1: The lesson is the test, and the reward is a sense of belonging.

Stage 2: The lesson is humility, and the reward is life.

Stage 3: The lesson is to know the Word and know your job, and the rewards are individual worth and value.

Stage 4: The lesson is to have a heart, and the reward is individual responsibility to support the group.

Stage 5: The lesson is to keep focus, and the rewards are rest, companions, protection, and contentment.

Stage 6: The lesson is enablement, and the reward is credibility.

Stage 7: The lesson is not to forget, and the reward is autonomy to lead and create.

Sense of Belonging—Stage Six

Philadelphia is the sixth city. That means we will use the sixth construct in the Ephesus model to help us understand and interpret the Scripture dealing with this church. Stage six of the Ephesus model states that the agent of first cause with authority and empowered members must shepherd the group into success. This will be the realization of a fulfilled hope.

The Lesson

In this city, Philadelphia, we will experience success. Through this success, we will realize our founding hope from stage two of the Ephesus model. The journey will not be for naught.

We got our rest in Sardis. We worked with the team in Thyatira. We proved ourselves individually in Pergamum. We received eternal life and provision for this life in Smyrna. We passed our test of belief and received a sense of belonging in Ephesus. We are ready for Philadelphia.

We see that Jesus holds the key of David (Revelation. 3:7). Since he immediately mentions doors three times, I presume this key of David can lock and unlock these doors. Either way, Jesus controls access. Philadelphia fulfills their obligations, and Jesus supports them. Jesus said as much (Revelation 3:8). Jesus enabled this church to succeed!

Philadelphia and Laodicea are different from the other churches in the greeting. The other five churches derived their greeting from Revelation 1:12–18. The churches of Philadelphia and Laodicea did not derive their greetings from this text. Their greeting texts are new to us.

1. **Greeting of Ephesus** Revelation 2:1: "Holds the seven stars in his right hand and walks among the seven golden lampstands" (derived from Revelation 1:12–13 and 16).

2. **Greeting of Smyrna** Revelation 2:8: "First and the Last, who died and came to life again" (derived from Revelation 1:17–18).

3. **Greeting of Pergamum** Revelation 2:12: "Has the sharp double-edged sword" (derived from Revelation 1:16).

4. **Greeting of Thyatira** Revelation 2:18: "Eyes like blazing fire and whose feet are like burnished bronze" (derived from Revelation 1:14–15).

5. **Greeting of Sardis** Revelation 3:1: "Holds the seven spirits of God and the seven stars" (derived from Revelation 1:16).

6. **Greeting of Philadelphia** Revelation 3:7: "Holy and true, who holds the key of David" (not derived from Revelation 1:12–18).

7. **Greeting of Laodicea** Revelation 3:14: "The Amen, the faithful and true witness, the ruler of God's creation" (not derived from Revelation 1:12–18).

I am not entirely sure of all the reasons the last two churches are different. There is a key difference in these last two churches, though. They are decentralized. Oppressive centralized state governments do not control these churches.

We still use the historical view that places the Philadelphia church around AD 1750 until the rapture (Larkin 1919, Lahaye 1999). During this time period, there were significant changes in the world. This is the time of the Age of Revolutions, Industrial Revolution, Age of Reason, and the Age of Enlightenment. All of these changes marked a power shift from a centralized authority to decentralized groups and individuals. This is a global paradigm shift.

The state-run churches were not immune to this fracturing force. Pergamum (AD 312–606[36]) was historically the first church to align itself with a secular government. This fused power-sharing relationship is an affront to God.[37] During this Philadelphian era, state-church power began to wane, and religious oligarchies began to lose their relevance.

Each church we have visited so far fell under an internal or external threat. Jesus protected this church from an external threat (Revelation 3:7–8). There is an incipient transition of power on the near horizon. The Philadelphian church will catalyze this spiritual transformation.

We know the church in Philadelphia did not have much strength (Revelation 3:8). The believers in this church age had small congregations and were in a minority status (Lahaye 1999). These true believers were under the thumb of the so-called church and its fraternal twin—the state. Both wielded near equal power. This near equal power-sharing relationship was manifested and strengthened centuries before when the Father of Europe, Charlemagne, was crowned as Emperor in AD 800 by Pope Leo III on Christmas Day.

---

36 Timothy Lahaye, *Revelation Unveiled* (Grand Rapids: Zondervan, 1999), 24.

37 Clarence Larkin, *The Book of Revelation: A Study of The Last Prophetic Book of Holy Scripture, Illustrated* (Philadelphia: Erwin W. Moyer Co. Printers, 1919), 22.

There were separate and sovereign civil and ecclesiastic laws and courts, but you could end up in the same common jail for crossing either. This is the age of the Recusants, Protestation Rolls, Dissenters, Nonconformists, Protestants, and Puritans. True Christians were often jailed for their beliefs for not holding the government sanctioned opinion. Through this, the Lord reminded them, "I have the Key of David."

The Lord was still the on-scene commander, in military speak. "I am in control, and the door of salvation is already open," God told them. It is no wonder the Great Awakening happened on this church's watch. This age was enabled to succeed.

This is an excerpt from a period contemporary author that demonstrates the struggle between the Philadelphian true church and the apostate state-controlled business called a church. From Joseph Besse's (1736) *A Full answer to the Country Parson's Plea Against the Quakers Tythe-Bill:*

> And in the year of our Lord 1540, and 31st of Henry the 8th's Reign, he summoned a solemn Parliament, to be holden at Westminster the 28th day of April, of all the States and Burgesses of the Realm; also, a Synod, or Convocation, of all the Archbishops, Bishops, and other learned Clergy of this Realm, to be in like manner assembled: In which Parliament, certain Articles were agreed to and published, in favour of the Popish Religion, but very grievous to the Protestants; commanding them, by the Authority of King and Parliament, on pain of Death, by Tortures and Burning, they should not, "by Word, Writing, Imprinting, Cyphering, or any otherwise, publish, preach, teach, say, affirm, declare, dispute, argue, or hold an Opinion, that in the Sacrament of the Alter, under form of Bread and Wine (after the Consecration thereof) there is not present really the Natural Body and Blood of our Saviour Jesus Christ.[38]

38   Joseph Besse, *A Full Answer To The Country Parson's Plea Against The Quakers Tythe-Bill, By The Author Of The Replication To The Country Parson's Papers and Plea* (Public Domain Reprint, Originally Printed in London, Printed for T. Cooper, at the Globe, 1736), 37.

Another excerpt (of hundreds available) from Joseph Besse's book verifies the active hostility the quasi-religious, quasi-political state-church took toward true believers who refused to contribute to their so-called church:

> This is not a bare Surmise; there are many Matters of Facts, both by Suits and Imprisonments–might be mentioned. But I will (at present) content myself with a few, which followeth:
>
> The First Instance.
>
> James Tuckett, in Devonshire, aged about 70 years who hath been blind upwards of 20 years, was prosecuted in Exchequer, by Parson Dodge, for a demand of 4l. 10s. (four pounds–ten shillings) on account of Tythes; and he not answering was committed to Exeter Gaol in May 1730, and continued a Prisoner till January 1735, being five Years and eight Months a close Prisoner.
>
> And about 9 Months after his Commitment, the said Parson Dodge filed another Bill against him in the Exchequer for the same Demand; to which his two Sons and a Daughter were made Parties–and this Suit doth yet continue against them all. –Here we plainly see the Leaven of Herod is at work–to put an old blind Man in Prison and soon after to prosecute his 3 Children, who were (in his Absence) the Support of his Family at home, and his own Support in Prison. Whether this be not the Fruits of a persecuting Spirit, judge ye.[39]

We know the Philadelphia church did not have much ecclesiastic strength, influence, or political clout (Revelation 3:8). The church was decentralized. Its people were purposely restricted from critical positions of authority. The people eventually protested their maltreatment and broke away from this tyranny.

When an enemy is centralized and possesses dominant power, the best counter tactic is likely a decentralized attack. Never assault the enemy where strengths are most relevant and effective. Effective

---

39   Ibid., 16.

insurgencies and clear-minded conventional armies both focus strategies on this point.

During the airborne drop of the 82nd and 101st Airborne Divisions in support of Operation Overlord, soldiers were scattered in a chaotic way in Normandy. Divisional, regimental, battalion, company, platoon, and squad integrity were compromised and nonexistent after the insertion operations. This required the NCOs and officers to form small *ad hoc* teams. This chaos set the conditions for the paratroops to succeed.

Some *ad hoc* teams had soldiers with 82nd double-A, All-American patches teamed up with soldiers wearing Screaming Eagle patches working together until unit cohesion could be reconstituted. These *ad hoc* decentralized teams conducting decentralized attacks became the undoing of the centralized, über-organized, über-structured German Wehrmacht on D-Day in Normandy. The configuration of the large, conventional, and unwieldy German units could not handle the swarms of tiny teams.

In the same respect, every rancher splitting fence posts knows that big logs split with little hits. Small, steady hits against a steel wedge and glut will slowly drive the wedge into a massive piece of wood until it cracks and divides. Big hits just bounce right off. This concept is counterintuitive. Philadelphia was the decentralized church—the church with little strength that split away from the powerful state-run churches and the centralized oligarchical churches with a thousand little hits of defiance.

The transition from the medieval to the early modern world was a not a smooth transition. In fact, this segue is notorious still today. This transition is coincident with the transition from the Sardis age to the Philadelphian age. The Middle Age's Great Pestilence is a key catalyst for this shift. "The Black Death was the trauma that liberated the new," wrote Norman Cantor.[40]

---

40   Norman F. Cantor, *In The Wake Of The Plague: The Black Death And The World It Made* (New York: Free Press, 2001, First Perennial Edition Published 2002), 202.

Just as the Baron's Magna Carta did not create overnight justice, the Great Pestilence did not create guild-partitioned yeomen or an educated middle class overnight. However, this middle class of yeomen did emerge. This new, educated, and entrepreneurial yeoman class would become the people who populated the church of the Philadelphian age. Due to printing technology, Scripture is now readily available to the masses in this age. The ability to search the Holy Scripture facilitates the common people's own true interpretation apart from political agenda. The people are now in a position to learn God's Word in an unfiltered setting without state-church intervention.

The previously powerless became enabled by possessing the Word of God. The common people became empowered—not just spiritually, but also economically and civilly. J. D. Tuckett corroborates this as fact. This transition of economic and civil power has spiritual overtones and will have significant implications as the controlling yoke of the state-church falls away.

J.D. Tuckett writes,

> This devastating pestilence, upon the whole, was favourable to the improvement of the laboring classes, inasmuch, as those who had escaped the devouring pestilence, were insufficient to discharge the ordinary duties of life; and to prevent the rise of wages above what the employer could afford to pay, an act of the legislature was passed.[41]

A new world is forming in this church's age. The transitions are not subtle. "In this twilight world between medieval feudalism an early modern capitalism ... some degree of individualism and a liberal sense of community was starting to creep in."[42]

---

41   J. D. Tuckett, *A History of the Past and Present State Of The Labouring Population: Including the Progress of Agriculture, Manufacturing and Commerce, Volume One* (London: printed for Longman, Brown, Green And Longmans, and Edward Nettleton, Bookseller, Plymouth, 1846), 54.

42   Norman F. Cantor, *In The Wake Of The Plague: The Black Death And The World It Made* (New York: Free Press, 2001, First Perennial Edition Published 2002), 99.

This "sense of community starting to creep in" Cantor describes is the proto sense of community (belonging) the Philadelphian church will build upon. This true church, the church of Philadelphia, represents a relationship restored with God and a host of saved souls to corroborate the claim. As a pendulum swings equidistant in two directions, the Great Pestilence's reciprocal is the Great Awakening. The Great Awakening would not have been possible without a companion test of equal amplitude.

Jeremiah Burroughs (born c.1600), a Puritan preacher, was a contemporary minister in the time of the plague. He raised questions about the devastation of the Great Pestilence that he experienced firsthand. In the gift to achieve understanding through suffering and tribulation, Burroughs was to the Great Pestilence what Viktor Frankl was to the Holocaust. "Whenever the plague or pestilence comes to those who are under such a promise (Psalm 91), it is for some special and notable work, and God requires them to search and examine in a special manner, to find out His meaning; there is so much to be learned in the promise (Psalm 91) that God has made concerning this particular evil, that the people of God may come to quiet and content their hearts in this affliction."[43]

Jeremiah Burroughs demonstrated unbelievable faith and understanding. He predated the Great Awakening, so he anxiously awaited a "special and notable work" he knew was forthcoming because of "this particular evil." Even when the promise of Psalm 91 (protection from pestilence) seemed unfulfilled, Burroughs remained faithful.

The incipient Philadelphia church and its "open door" (Revelation 3:8) symbolize the Great Awakening that was just over the horizon and unable to be seen in the time of Jeremiah Burroughs in the mid-1600s. However, Burroughs sensed the winds of greatness blowing in what we came to know as the Great Awakening. This generation, that of the Philadelphian church, would be an age for the books.

---

43   Jeremiah Burroughs, *Rare Jewel of Christian Contentment* (Wilmington: Sovereign Grace Publishers, 1971, 1999), 26–27.

This was not the first time in history that plague (pestilence) released a people from tyranny. Of course, the ten plagues caused Pharaoh to release the children of Israel to Moses (Exodus 7–11, Habakkuk 3:1–6).

The Reward of Philadelphia

Through historical events, we can see how the small and dispersed congregations of the Philadelphia churches were able to succeed. This lesson brought them to the place of reward (Revelation 3:12). There is a common denominator here—names. This verse and this city are all about names. This seven-verse text for Philadelphia uses the word *name* four times; this is significant. This is part of the basis for the discovery of the sixth component of God's method of order.

We need to know that we can make a name for ourselves. We need recognition among our peers. This is how we achieve credibility. We must know we have value, we matter, we can support the team in a relevant way, and others will recognize our contributions. This is our reputation. It is our name.

This recognition should be a sincere public recognition. The acknowledgement does not necessarily need to be a formal presentation but a genuine recognition that all know is real and deserved. If an award or recognition is given and received that is undeserved, it devalues the credibility of all past, present, and future awards from that source. Rank and file can spot a phony in a second. McMillan and Chavis express this lesson and reward in a secular context. "We believe too that feelings of belonging and emotional safety lead to self-investment in the community, which has the consequence of giving a member the sense of having earned his or her membership."[44]

I am actually amazed at how close secular thinkers are to God's plan. There are differences, of course. The order is not the same, and the lesson of Smyrna is missing, along with Christ's role as a redeemer.

---

44   David W. McMillan and David M. Chavis, "Sense of Community: A Definition and Theory," *Journal of Community Psychology* Vol. 14 (January 1986): 15.

Nevertheless, they are very similar. I believe both parties are onto something. Below, I diagram this last sentence with respect to what we have learned from our churches in God's method of order.

We believe too that *feelings of belonging* (reward of Ephesus) and *emotional safety* (reward of Sardis) lead to *self-investment* (reward of Pergamum) in the *community* (reward of Thyatira), which has the consequence of giving a member the *sense of having earned his or her membership* (reward of Philadelphia).[45]

Maslow characterizes this concept as "being useful and necessary in the world."[46] We do need to know that we are useful. We need to receive that recognition among our peers. God knows this. He spells it out in the reward of Philadelphia.

Without relevance, we wither. We must strive through the cities in sequence to earn our place here. Any hint of elevation apart from actual ability will create friction and dissent.

We have one more city to travel to and one more central lesson with one more reward. This destination will have the best reward of all the cities.

Laodicea is our last church and our final destination. There will be no need to leave from here. You will have arrived.

---

45   Ibid.

46   A. H. Maslow, "A Theory of Human Motivation," *Classics in the History of Psychology,* posted August 2000, http://psychclassics.yorku.ca/Maslow/motivation.htm.

CHAPTER 7

The Churches: Laodicea

Remember your Creator in the days of your
youth, before the days of trouble come

—Ecclesiastes 12:1

Immeasurable Love: Come, ye aged saints, be children again; and
you that have long known your Lord, take up your first spelling
book, and go over your A B C again, by learning that God so
loved the world, that He gave His Son to die, that man might live
through Him. I do not call you to an elementary lesson because
you have forgotten your letters, but because it is a good thing to
refresh the memory, and a blessed thing to feel young again. [47]

—Charles H. Spurgeon (1834–1892)

Welcome to Laodicea

This is our last city, and the lesson here will tie all the previous lessons
together. Our reward here is opulent and underserved.

Laodicea's central lesson and reward are under the headings
Remembering and *Autonomy*. The lesson is do not forget your previous

---

[47]   Roger P. Elwood, Comp., *Immeasurable Love, Charles Spurgeon, Great Sermons
Volume One* (Uhrichsville: Barbour Publishing, 1998), 64.

lessons, and the reward is autonomy (authority) to create and lead. Let us get going and go meet the people of the seventh and last church!

Revelation 3:14-21 was written to the church in Laodicea:

> To the angel of the church in Laodicea write: These are the words of the Amen, the faithful and true witness, the ruler of God's creation. I know your deeds, that you are neither cold nor hot. I wish you were either one or the other! So, because you are lukewarm—neither hot nor cold—I am about to spit you out of my mouth. You say, "I am rich; I have acquired wealth and do not need a thing." But you do not realize that you are wretched, pitiful, poor, blind and naked. I counsel you to buy from me gold refined in the fire, so you can become rich; and white clothes to wear, so you can cover your shameful nakedness; and salve to put on your eyes, so you can see.
>
> Those whom I love I rebuke and discipline. So be earnest, and repent. Here I am! I stand at the door and knock. If anyone hears my voice and opens the door, I will come in and eat with him, and he with me. To him who overcomes, I will give the right to sit with me on the throne, just as I overcame and sat down with my Father on his throne. He who has an ear, let him hear what the Spirit says to the churches.

Outline

The Stages of the Ephesus Model—Sense of Belonging

Stage 1: The lesson is the test, and the reward is a sense of belonging.

Stage 2: The lesson is humility, and the reward is life.

Stage 3: The lesson is to know the Word and know your job, and the rewards are individual worth and value.

Stage 4: The lesson is to have a heart, and the reward is individual responsibility to support the group.

Stage 5: The lesson is to keep focus, and the rewards are rest, companions, protection, and contentment.

Stage 6: The lesson is enablement, and the reward is credibility.

Stage 7: The lesson is not to forget, and the reward is autonomy to lead and create.

Sense of Belonging—Stage Seven

Laodicea is the seventh city. That means we will use the seventh construct in the Ephesus model to help us understand and interpret the Scripture dealing with this church. Stage seven of the Ephesus model states that a legacy translates into a shared history.

This is the last city we will visit. This church will tie together all the lessons and rewards we have gained along this journey. In stage one, the agent of first cause established criteria to define a group. In stage two, we decided the agent of first cause was legitimate; therefore, the proposed group is also legitimate. We placed our hopes in the shared purpose of the group. In stage three, we endured faithfully in our individual role to support the group. This creates lasting bonds with other members and with the greater entity. In stage four, we as individuals received reciprocating love and support from the group. In stage five, we kept focus and corrected course to remain relevant in the changing conditions of our environments. In stage six, our hopes of success from stage two were realized.

This last stage is the stage of our legacy. In this stage of a sense of belonging, the members will find very deep meaning in the continuity of a shared past. As the organization perpetuates itself through the generations, the present members will find that the same cords of meaning and purpose that connected the hearts of the charter members connect their hearts as well.

This continuity of meaning can be seen in a legacy car company. The workers may find purpose and meaning in building cars for the same company that produced icons of Americana. The workers share a past with purpose and meaning; they derive their identity from this legacy. Imagine the organization if one day the company quit producing cars and trucks. Instead, the company leaders make a surprise announcement to shed this legacy of car production and enter the lumber business. How would that affect the identity of the company and its workers? People outside the organization would view this decision as schizophrenic leadership. Chaos would be the natural result.

This shared history is the same connection a genealogist may feel when discovering his or her family history, which is also his or her own story. Connection to the past may be felt when a congregation sings an ancient hymn of worship. This hymn connects the members to past generations and an ancient God. This connection provides comfort and meaning to the people.

The leaders of our groups are responsible to the past members to maintain a continuous legacy for the current members. This continuity of identity ties together all the stages of a sense of belonging. There is deep scriptural truth in maintaining a continuous legacy with purpose.

Revelation 3:14 reveals this scriptural truth. In this verse, Jesus revealed himself as the Amen, the faithful and true witness and ruler of God's creation. *Amen* means "so be it." Jesus said, "This is the final word." Jesus is the faithful and true witness, so we know there is continuity in his message. He is the ruler of God's creation. Here, we know that his continuity goes all the way back to the beginning. Remember that in stage seven of a sense of belonging, the current members must have unity of purpose and meaning with the charter members. Jesus advertised as much in this verse. God is always the same.

This stage of a sense of belonging leads us to our central lesson of Laodicea. The lesson is not to forget what you have learned. Keep what you have learned in the seven cities in practice.

The Lesson

We must commit to remember. How do we know that *remembering* is what the passage is trying to tell us? The Lord identified himself as the ruler of God's creation! After this entire journey, if there is one thing we should know, it is that God is the Creator, and he rules his own creation. In stage one of our sense of belonging, God defined the criteria for the formation of the identity of the church. He did, after all, enable us to succeed while we were in Philadelphia. We interpret his order, not our own, in this journey. How can we forget that?

God would not have alluded to remembering, except we all know he is completely right. We forget all the time. When things go well, we do not give God his rightful respect or proper place in our lives. We do not pray or worship him as we ought to. Through Jesus, we have our legacy spiritual connection to all the churches of every age. This legacy is the essence of our sense of belonging to God. God is eternal; he does not require this legacy. Legacy is for the people. However, we glorify God through the legacy we experience.

Look at Revelation 3:15. The Bible says, "I know your deeds, that you are neither cold nor hot. I wish you were either one or the other!" This seems to be an out-of-place statement from the Lord. He would rather this church be against him than be uncaring and lukewarm?

In 2002, I was stationed in the Sinai of Egypt in support of the MFO (Multi-national Force and Observers) with Task Force 2-153 to monitor the Camp David Accords from September of 1978 between Egypt and Israel. There was a retired Command Sergeant Major from the US Army Special Forces community who worked there as a civilian. I periodically dropped by and talked to him where he worked on base in the gymnasium. I talked to him about his days in Vietnam and his experiences, and he showed me pictures that he kept from his time in that country. One of the pictures he showed me was an empty bamboo makeshift hut or jail. He said his unit captured members of the Viet Cong (VC) and detained them in these huts for questioning.

The Command Sergeant Major said there were two types of prisoners: those who just cried and fell to pieces because they were captured, and those who were defiant. The prisoners who fell to pieces were of no operational value to the US forces or the VC. The defiant prisoners, however, were of value. He said they tried to reason with these guys in order to get them to see the ultimate gain they would receive for their nation to resist communism and switch sides.

This is what the Lord means by being lukewarm. Even if you are on the wrong team, at least you have enough spine to get on a team. If you are just going to sob in the corner or not completely choose a side, you are not much value to anyone. Commitment is another way of thinking of the concept. If you are willing to commit, then the Lord at least has a starting point to attempt a SAR (search and rescue) mission if you are lost. Otherwise, we would just be a nebulous mish-mash of nothingness—no grid, no quadrant, and no place from which to realistically initiate recovery plans.

Being true (committing) to our original purpose will connect us to the meaning of our past. Shared history is a critical component of a sense of belonging. Without a shared past, what would we connect to? Remembering is a touchstone quality in the Ephesus model. This lesson brings all our lessons under one roof. Stage seven of the Ephesus model generates continuity through unity by remembering the past. "A nation reveals itself not only by the men it produces but also by the men it honors, the men it remembers."[48] This lesson leads us to our final reward.

The Reward of Laodicea

We will sit and eat with the Lord, and he gives us autonomy here. In Laodicea, real people will share in the throne and sovereignty of the Father. This is absolutely over-the-top and unexpected, because we are not always the best stewards. We could tear up a steel ball with a rubber mallet, but God still falls in love with us anyway.

Laodicea is the worst bunch yet, and the courtship continues and culminates in marriage. The Lord has nothing good to say about this

---

48   John F. Kennedy. "Remarks at Amherst College (October 26, 1963)," accessed June 23, 2013. http://millercenter.org/president/speeches/detail/3379.

church. Its people are slick and smug. Unfortunately, we are *like them.* This is today's church. God still claims us. He will not betray (or forget) our lesson of Ephesus. We still belong to him, and he readily claims us as his own. He stands by us, even when we hardly deserve his favor.

Who does that? That is how good God is. It is unbelievable. Look back at how God got to know us. In Ephesus, he offered us the Tree of Life (Revelation 2:7). It is almost as if he said to us, "You guys go outside and pick some fruit off the big tree in the middle of the field." No sooner do we get out of earshot than God asks the nearest angel, "So, who were those guys anyway?" Then in Pergamum, he warmed up to us. He brought us some manna (Revelation 2:17). Things seem to be a little less awkward. By the time we get to Laodicea, he is crazy in love with us. He sits and eats with us, and we know the marriage supper of the Lamb is yet to come (Revelation 19:9)! He gives us his throne![49]

The throne is an actual throne, but it also has symbolic meaning for us now on earth. The reward of Laodicea gives us room to have autonomy to lead and create. We strive to achieve autonomy and a certain amount of sovereignty in the context of our families, jobs, and organizations. This is how we express our creativity, solve difficult problems, and establish future goals and priorities. This is a mark of trust and accomplishment of the most capable among us. This reward is a culminating reward, proven and rightfully given through the acquisition of the previous six rewards.

The autonomy we gain in Laodicea actually replaces the autonomy we surrendered in Smyrna where we acknowledged God's holiness as legitimate. This system of exchange is counterintuitive, but this trade is normal inside the mystery of God's spiritual economy (Matthew 10:39). Matthew 16:13–19 highlights this exchange when Simon Peter acknowledges Jesus as the Christ. Peter then receives his sanction to build the church.

---

49   See also 2 Peter 1:1-4 and 1 Corinthians 6:2-3. God shares his sovereignty with us.

The collective lessons of traveling through all the churches and cities in sequential order is like the lesson we learned from Eve in Genesis about God getting to know us first. Maybe this is the way God allows us space and time to get to know him, building upon Israel Zangwill's idea of the choosing chosen concept. This allowance of grace only happens with God. He is good to us, and his ways draw us to him. The reclamation may be an event, but it is most likely accomplished through process.

This grace shows how the Lord is on our side and wants us to succeed. He knows that apart from his order, we will not meet our potential. Therefore, he continuously draws us to him. This drawing and wooing of the Lord starts the journey. He wants us to have faith and believe him. Faith is the first step. Faith is how you can gain a sense of belonging to the Lord. Belief is our greatest opportunity.

Jonathan Edwards (1703–1758), in his sermon "Sinners in the Hands of an Angry God," said,

> Unconverted men walk over the pit of hell on a rotten covering, and there are innumerable places in the covering so weak that they will not bear their weight, and these places are not seen. The arrows of death fly unseen at noonday; the sharpest sight cannot discern them. God has so many different unsearchable ways of taking wicked men out of the world and sending them to hell, that there is nothing to make it appear, that God had need to be at the expense of a miracle, or go out of the ordinary course of His providence, to destroy any wicked man, at any moment … And now you have an extraordinary opportunity, a day wherein Christ has thrown the door of mercy wide open, and stands in calling and crying with a loud voice to poor sinners; a day wherein many are flocking to Him, and pressing into the kingdom of God.[50]

50   Roger P. Elwood, Comp., *Sinners in the Hands of an Angry God, Jonathan Edwards, Great Sermons Volume One* (Uhrichsville: Barbour Publishing, 1998), 15, 26.

Consolidate Your Learning

Method of Order

Table 2

Ephesus	God is holy; that is the criterion for our test of belief. We accept his offer, choosing to belong to him and worship him, since we know that we are far from holy.
Smyrna	With a contrite attitude, we submit to God's authority in our lives. Our hope is in Jesus. He sustains our lives throughout eternity.
Pergamum	We study God's Word to develop ourselves. We continue to learn and grow in competence and acumen in preparation for our next assignments.
Thyatira	We must use our gifts and skills we developed as subordinates inside the group. This will prepare us to be leaders of the group when we are ready and capable to lead.
Sardis	Stay on track, and keep focus; keep working. In Jesus, we will have rest, companionship, protection, and contentment.
Philadelphia	God will enable us to succeed. We need recognition as credible, relevant, and honorable contributors to establish a name for ourselves among our peers. Our hopes need fulfillment. This legitimizes the trip we took in the first place.
Laodicea	Do not forget what you have learned! The most capable will be given autonomy to lead and create. We all need a share of glory and sovereignty.

CHAPTER 8

The Proofs: Fifteen Corroborating Examples of God's Method of Order in Scripture

Example 1

Genesis 1:27–30

The Cultural Mandate

1. **Reward of Ephesus:** sense of belonging. Genesis 1:27: "So God created man in his own image, in the image of God he created him; male and female he created them."

2. **Reward of Smyrna:** life. Genesis 1:28: God blessed them and said to them, "Be fruitful and increase in number."

3. **Reward of Pergamum:** individual responsibility and worth. Genesis 1:28: "Fill the earth and subdue it."[51]

4. **Reward of Thyatira:** responsibility to the group. Genesis 1:28–30: "Rule over the fish of the sea and the birds of the air and over every living creature that moves on the ground. Then God said, 'I give you every seed-bearing plant on the face of the whole earth and every tree that has fruit with seed in it. They will be yours for food. And to all the beasts of the earth and all the birds of the air and all the creatures

---

51   Genesis 1:28 is also known as the "cultural mandate." This is our sacred responsibility to contribute practically to society as just stewards.

that move on the ground—everything that has the breath of life in it—I give every green plant for food.'"[52]

5. **Reward of Sardis:** rest, protection, companionship, and contentment. Genesis 1:30: "And it was so." (This is space and time to grow normally—contentment.)

Example 2

Exodus 2:15–25, 3

Moses' Exile

1. **Reward of Ephesus:** sense of belonging. After an act of kindness to Jethro's daughters, Jethro took Moses in from the wilderness.

2. **Reward of Smyrna:** life. Jethro gave Moses food. He also gave Moses his daughter, Zippporah, as his wife. Moses and Zipporah had a son.

3. **Reward of Pergamum:** individual responsibility and worth. Jethro provided Moses with an occupation as a shepherd.

4. **Reward of Thyatira:** responsibility to the group. In the burning bush, God provided Moses with a mission to deliver the Hebrew people.

5. **Reward of Sardis:** rest, protection, companionship, and contentment. Moses expressed concern to God about his new role. God promised to be with Moses.

6. **Reward of Philadelphia:** credibility and a name. Exodus 3:13–15: "Moses said to God, 'Suppose I go to the Israelites and say to them, "The God of your fathers has sent me to you," and they ask me, "What is his name?" Then what shall I tell them?' God said to Moses, 'I AM WHO I AM. This is what you are to say to the Israelites: "I am has sent me to you."' God also said to Moses, 'Say to the Israelites, "The

---

52   This excerpt has greater implications for how we organize our work. Agricultural responsibility is an allegory to communicate the point.

Lord, the God of your fathers—the God of Abraham, the God of Isaac and the God of Jacob—has sent me to you." This is my name forever, the name by which I am to be remembered from generation to generation.'"

7. **Reward of Laodicea:** autonomy to create and lead; sovereignty. Moses began the process that would culminate in the people's freedom.

Example 3

Exodus 20

The Ten Commandments

1. **Reward of Ephesus:** sense of belonging. Verses 1–12 deal with our vertical relationships of belonging to God and our parents. Exodus 20:1-4, 7-8, 12: "And God spoke all these words: I am the Lord your God, who brought you out of Egypt, out of the land of slavery. You shall have no other gods before me. You shall not make for yourself an idol ... You shall not misuse the name of the Lord ... Remember the Sabbath day by keeping it holy ... Honor your father and your mother."

2. **Reward of Smyrna:** life. Exodus 20:12: "So that you may live long in the land the Lord your God is giving you."

3. **Reward of Pergamum:** individual responsibility and worth. Exodus 20:13-15: "You shall not murder. You shall not commit adultery. You shall not steal."

4. **Reward of Thyatira:** responsibility to the group. Exodus 20:16-17: "You shall not give false testimony against your neighbor. You shall not covet your neighbor's house. You shall not covet your neighbor's wife, or his manservant or maidservant, his ox or donkey, or anything that belongs to your neighbor."

5. Reward of Sardis: rest, protection, companionship, and contentment. Exodus 20:20: "Do not be afraid, God has come to test you, so that the fear of God will be with you to keep you from sinning."

Example 4

Leviticus 26:9–13

Moses' Reward for Obedience and Address to the People

1. Reward of Ephesus: sense of belonging. Leviticus 26:9: "I will look on you with favor."

2. Reward of Smyrna: life. Leviticus 26:9: "And make you fruitful and increase your numbers."

3. Reward of Pergamum: individual responsibility and worth. Leviticus 26:9: "And I will keep my covenant with you." (God fulfills the individual's role.)

4. Reward of Thyatira: responsibility to the group. Leviticus 26:10: "You will still be eating last year's harvest when you will have to move it out to make room for the new."[53]

5. Reward of Sardis: rest, protection, companionship, and contentment. Leviticus 26:11–12: "I will put my dwelling place among you, and I will not abhor you. I will walk among you and be your God."[54]

6. Reward of Philadelphia: credibility and a name. Leviticus 26:12: "And you will be my people."[55]

---

53   Collective agricultural labor is an allegory for corporate responsibilities we owe to the group.

54   *Walk* was used in Revelation 3:4 in the Sardis church as well. Walking in this context is an allegory or symbol that signifies close friendship, protection, and communion with the Lord.

55   This gives the Jews their rightful identity of God's legitimate people. See the Lesson of Thyatira—Rosenthal and Zangwill in Chapter 4.

7. **Reward of Laodicea:** autonomy to create and lead; sovereignty. Leviticus 26:13: "I am the Lord your God, who brought you out of Egypt so that you would no longer be slaves to the Egyptians; I broke the bars of your yoke and enabled you to walk with heads held high."

Example 5

Deuteronomy 6:1-12

The Shema

1. **Reward of Ephesus:** sense of belonging. Deuteronomy 6:1-2: "These are the commands, decrees and laws the Lord your God directed me to teach you to observe in the land that you are crossing the Jordan to possess, so that you, your children and their children after them may fear the Lord your God as long as you live by keeping all his decrees and commands that I give you."

2. **Reward of Smyrna:** life. Deuteronomy 6:2: "And so that you may enjoy long life."

3. **Reward of Pergamum:** individual responsibility and worth. Deuteronomy 6:3-5: "Hear, O Israel, and be careful to obey so that it may go well with you and that you may increase greatly in a land flowing with milk and honey, just as the Lord, the God of your fathers, promised you. Hear, O Israel: The Lord our God. The Lord is one. Love the Lord your God with all your heart and with all your soul and with all your strength."

4. **Reward of Thyatira:** responsibility to the group. Deuteronomy 6:6-9: "These commandments that I give you today are to be upon your hearts.[56] Impress them on your children. Talk about them when you sit at home and when you walk along the road, when you lie down and when you get up. Tie them as symbols on your hands and

---

56   A key lesson of Thyatira—lead with a heart.

bind them on your foreheads. Write them on the doorframes of your houses and on your gates."

5. **Reward of Sardis:** rest, protection, companionship, and contentment. Deuteronomy 6:10–11: "When the Lord your God brings you into the land he swore to your fathers, to Abraham, Isaac and Jacob, to give you–a land with large, flourishing cities you did not build, houses filled with all kinds of good things you did not provide, wells you did not dig, and vineyards and olive groves you did not did not plant …"

6. **Reward of Philadelphia:** credibility and a name. Deuteronomy 6:11: "Then when you eat and are satisfied."[57]

7. **Reward of Laodicea:** autonomy to create and lead; sovereignty. Deuteronomy 6:12: "Be careful that you do not forget the Lord, who brought you out of Egypt, out of the land of slavery."[58]

Example 6

Deuteronomy 28:1–14

Moses' Blessings of Obedience and Address to the People

1. **Reward of Ephesus:** sense of belonging. Deuteronomy 28:1–3: "If you fully obey the Lord your God and carefully follow all his commands I give you today, the Lord your God will set you high above all the nations on earth. All these blessings will come upon you and accompany you if you obey the Lord your God. You will be blessed in the city and blessed in the country."

2. **Reward of Smyrna:** life. Deuteronomy 28:4–5: "The fruit of your womb will be blessed, and the crops of your land and the young of

---

57   The safety, contentment, and notoriety Israel received from God's provision corroborated this promise, giving credibility to God's Word and God's people. If they were ill taken care of by God, they would be the opposite of credible.

58   The lesson from Laodicea is not to forget!

your livestock—the calves of your herds and the lambs of your flocks. Your basket and your kneading trough will be blessed."

3. **Reward of Pergamum:** individual responsibility and worth. Deuteronomy 28:6: "You will be blessed when you come in and blessed when you go out."[59]

4. **Reward of Thyatira:** responsibility to the group. Deuteronomy 28:7-8: "The Lord will grant that the enemies who rise up against you will be defeated before you. They will come at you from one direction but flee from you in seven. The Lord will send a blessing on your barns and on everything you put your hand to. The Lord your God will bless you in the land he is giving you."[60]

5. **Reward of Sardis:** rest, protection, companionship, and contentment. Deuteronomy 28:9: "The Lord will establish you as his holy people, as he promised you on oath, if you keep the commands of the Lord your God and walk in his ways."[61]

6. **Reward of Philadelphia:** credibility and a name. Deuteronomy 28:10-12: "Then all the peoples on earth will see that you are called by the name of the Lord, and they will fear you. The Lord will grant you abundant prosperity–in the fruit of your womb, the young of your livestock and the crops of your ground–in the land he swore to your forefathers to give you. The Lord will open the heavens, the storehouses of his bounty, to send rain on your land in season and to bless all the work of your hands. You will lend to many nations but will borrow from none."

7. **Reward of Laodicea:** autonomy to create and lead; sovereignty. Deuteronomy 28:13: "The Lord will make you the head, not the tail. If

---

59   "Going in and going out" is a way of saying "day-to-day affairs." This language is used as an allegory for individual responsibilities.

60   Collective martial and agricultural responsibilities are used as allegories for all corporate responsibilities.

61   *Walk* was used in Revelation 3:4 in regard to the Sardis church; it was also used in the Leviticus 26 example. Walking in this context is an allegory or a symbol that signifies close friendship, protection, and communion with the Lord.

you pay attention to the commands of the Lord your God that I give you this day and carefully follow them, you will always be at the top, never at the bottom."[62]

Example 7

Ruth 4:13–17

The Story of Ruth and Boaz

1. **Reward of Ephesus:** sense of belonging. Ruth 4:13: "So Boaz took Ruth and she became his wife."

2. **Reward of Smyrna:** life. Ruth 4:13: "Then he went to her, and the Lord enabled her to conceive, and she gave birth to a son."

3. **Reward of Pergamum:** individual responsibility and worth. Ruth 4:14: "The women said to Naomi: Praise be to the Lord, who this day has not left you without a kinsman-redeemer. May he become famous throughout Israel!"

4. **Reward of Thyatira:** responsibility to the group. Ruth 4:15: "He will renew your life and sustain you in your old age. For your daughter-in-law, who loves you and who is better to you than seven sons, has given him birth."

5. **Reward of Sardis:** rest, protection, companionship, and contentment. Ruth 4:16: "Then Naomi took the child, laid him in her lap and cared for him."

6. **Reward of Philadelphia:** credibility and a name. Ruth 4:17: "The women living there said, Naomi has a son. And they named him Obed."

7. **Reward of Laodicea:** autonomy to create and lead; sovereignty. Ruth 4:17: "He was the father of Jesse, the father of David (King David)."[63]

---

62 "Pay attention" is another way of saying "do not forget"—the key lesson of Laodicea.

63 King David was used as an analogue to represent the reward of Laodicea. David embodied autonomy and sovereignty.

Example 8

First Kings 8–9

King Solomon's Prayer to Dedicate the Temple

1. **Reward of Ephesus:** sense of belonging. First Kings 8:22–24: "Then Solomon stood before the alter of the Lord in front of the whole assembly of Israel, spread out his hands toward heaven and said: O Lord, God of Israel, there is no God like you in heaven above or on earth below—you who keep your covenant of love with your servants who continue wholeheartedly in your way. You have kept your promise to your servant David my father; with your mouth you have promised and with your hand you have fulfilled it—as it is today."

2. **Reward of Smyrna:** life. First Kings 8:35–36: "When the heavens are shut up and there is no rain because your people have sinned against you, and when they pray toward this place and confess your name and turn from their sin because you have afflicted them, then hear from heaven and forgive the sin of your servants, your people Israel. Teach them the right way to live, and send rain on the land you gave your people for an inheritance."[64]

3. **Reward of Pergamum:** individual responsibility and worth. First Kings 8:39: "Forgive and act; deal with each man according to all he does, since you know his heart (for you alone know the hearts of all men)."

4. **Reward of Thyatira:** responsibility to the group. First Kings 8:44–45: "When your people go to war against their enemies, wherever you send them, and when they pray to the Lord toward the city you have chosen and the temple I have built for your Name, then hear from heaven their prayer and their plea, and uphold their cause."[65]

5. **Reward of Sardis:** rest, protection, companionship, and contentment. First Kings 8:56–58: "Praise be to the Lord, who has given rest to his

---

64   Having a contrite attitude toward God is one of our lessons from Smyrna.

65   Collective martial responsibilities are used as an allegory for all corporate responsibilities.

people Israel just as he promised. Not one word has failed of all the good promises he gave through his servant Moses. May the Lord our God be with us as he was with our fathers; may he never leave us nor forsake us. May he turn our hearts to him, to walk in all his ways."[66]

6. **Reward of Philadelphia:** credibility and a name. First Kings 9:3: "The Lord said to him: 'I have heard the prayer and plea you have made before me; I have consecrated this temple, which you have built, by putting my Name there forever. My eyes and my heart will always be there.'"

7. **Reward of Laodicea:** autonomy to create and lead; sovereignty. First Kings 9:4–5: "As for you, if you walk before me in integrity of heart and uprightness, as David your father did, and do all I command and observe my decrees and laws, I will establish your royal throne over Israel forever, as I promised David your father when I said, 'You shall never fail to have a man on the throne of Israel.'"

Example 9

Esther 2:17–23, 6:1–6

Esther's Coronation

1. **Reward of Ephesus:** sense of belonging. Esther became the wife of King Xerxes, and he crowns Esther as the nation's queen.

2. **Reward of Smyrna:** life. King Xerxes gave a great banquet in Esther's honor.

3. **Reward of Pergamum:** individual responsibility and worth. Esther fulfilled her individual responsibilities by following Mordecai's (her adoptive father) instructions to the letter as a child and adult. She also listened to Hegai, the king's eunuch, and followed his advice.

---

66 *Walk* was used in Revelation 3:4 in reference to the Sardis church; it was also used in the Leviticus 26 and Deuteronomy 28 examples. *Walking* in this context is an allegory or symbol that signifies close friendship, protection, and communion with the Lord.

4. **Reward of Thyatira:** responsibility to the group. Mordecai discovered a plot to assassinate the king, and he disclosed the plot to Queen Esther. Queen Esther in return fulfilled her obligation to her family and nation by reporting the plot to the king.

5. **Reward of Sardis:** rest, protection, companionship, and contentment. The king's life was protected. The nation's contentment remained intact, since the coup was thwarted.

6. **Reward of Philadelphia:** credibility and a name. Scribes recorded Mordecai's name in the book of annals for protecting the king's life.

7. **Reward of Laodicea:** autonomy to create and lead; sovereignty. King Xerxes rewarded Mordecai with a signet ring, royal robe, royal horse, and royal crest.

Example 10

Job 1

Job's Tests

1. **Reward of Ephesus:** sense of belonging. Job 1:6–22 tells us of test one of two. Satan's first test against Job was an attempt to shatter his foundational sense of belonging. Satan attacked the things God gave to Job—his family and property—in order to get him to denounce God. Job's wife eventually cracked; she blamed God. Job remained faithful.

2. **Reward of Smyrna:** life. Job 2:1–9 tells us of test two of two. Satan attacked Job's health. Satan was not given authority to take Job's life, but he was allowed to harm Job physically. These two tests are topically and sequentially consistent with the method of order discovered and revealed in this book. Satan knows what is most important to us and subsequently where to concentrate an attack.

Example 11

Psalm 23

A Psalm of David

1. **Reward of Ephesus:** sense of belonging. Psalm 23:1: "The Lord is my shepherd."

2. **Reward of Smyrna:** life. Psalm 23:1: "I shall not be in want" We have no wants, since we are provided for.

3. **Reward of Pergamum:** individual responsibility and worth. Psalm 23:2: "He makes me lie down in green pastures." "Makes me" is an individual task and admission of worth from the Father through active care.

4. **Reward of Thyatira:** responsibility to the group. Psalm 23:2–3: "He leads me beside quiet waters, he restores my soul. He guides me in paths of righteousness for his name's sake." The Father receives glory through the righteousness of others in the group. Individuals support the collective.

5. **Reward of Sardis:** rest, protection, companionship, and contentment. Psalm 23:4: "Even though I walk through the valley of the shadow of death, I will fear no evil, for you are with me; your rod and your staff they comfort me."[67]

6. **Reward of Philadelphia:** credibility and a name. Psalm 23:5: "You prepare a table before me in the presence of my enemies."

7. **Reward of Laodicea:** autonomy to create and lead; sovereignty. Psalm 23:5–6: "You anoint my head with oil: my cup overflows. Surely goodness and love will follow me all the days of my life, and I will dwell in the house of the Lord forever."

---

67   *Walk* was used in Revelation 3:4 in reference to the Sardis church; it was also used in the Leviticus 26, Deuteronomy 28, and Solomon's dedication prayer examples (1 Kings 8). Walking in this context is an allegory or symbol that signifies close friendship, protection, and communion with the Lord.

Example 12

Psalm 103

A Psalm of David

1. **Reward of Ephesus:** sense of belonging. Psalm 103:1–3: "Praise the Lord, O my soul; all my inmost being, praise his holy name. Praise the Lord, O my soul, and forget not all his benefits—who forgives all your sins."

2. **Reward of Smyrna:** life. Psalm 103:3–5: "And heals all your diseases, who redeems your life from the pit and crowns you with love and compassion, who satisfies your desires with good things so that your youth is renewed like the eagle's."

3. **Reward of Pergamum:** individual responsibility and worth. Psalm 103:6–7: "The Lord works righteousness and justice for all the oppressed. He made known his ways to Moses."[68]

4. **Reward of Thyatira:** responsibility to the group. Psalm 103:7: "His deeds to the people of Israel."

5. **Reward of Sardis:** rest, protection, companionship, and contentment. Psalm 103:8–14: "The Lord is compassionate and gracious, slow to anger, abounding in love. He will not always accuse, nor will he harbor his anger forever; he does not treat us as our sins deserve or repay us according to our iniquities. For as high as the heavens are above the earth, so great is his love for those who fear him; as far as the east is from the west, so far has he removed our transgressions from us. As a father has compassion on his children, so the Lord has compassion on those who fear him; for he knows how we are formed, he remembers that we are dust."

6. **Reward of Philadelphia:** credibility and a name. Psalm 103:15–17: "As for man, his days are like grass, he flourishes like a flower of the field; the wind blows over it and it is gone, and its place remembers

---

68   Moses was an individual—the most humble man who ever lived (Numbers 12:3). Moses is an analogue for all individuals in the context that we all have individual roles to fulfill and are valuable and relevant.

it no more. But from everlasting to everlasting the Lord's love is with those who fear him, and his righteousness with their children's children."

7. **Reward of Laodicea:** autonomy to create and lead; sovereignty. Psalm 103:18-22: "With those who keep his covenant and remember to obey his precepts.[69] The Lord has established his throne in heaven, and his kingdom rules over all. Praise the Lord, you his angels, you mighty ones who do his bidding, who obey his word. Praise the Lord, all his heavenly hosts, you his servants who do his will. Praise the Lord, all his works everywhere in his dominion. Praise the Lord O my soul."

Example 13

Psalm 111

A Psalm of David

1. **Reward of Ephesus:** sense of belonging. Psalm 111:1-4: "Praise the Lord. I will extol the Lord with all my heart in the council of the upright and in the assembly. Great are the works of the Lord; they are pondered by all who delight in them. Glorious and majestic are his deeds, and his righteousness endures forever. He has caused his wonders to be remembered; the Lord is gracious and compassionate."

2. **Reward of Smyrna:** life. Psalm 111:5: "He provides food for those who fear him."

3. **Reward of Pergamum:** individual responsibility and worth. Psalm 111:5: "He remembers his covenant forever." (Like Example 4, God fulfills the individual role.)

4. **Reward of Thyatira:** responsibility to the group. Psalm 111:6-8: "He has shown his people the power of his works, giving them the lands of other nations. The works of his hands are faithful and just; all his

---

69   Our lesson from Laodicea is not to forget!

precepts are trustworthy. They are steadfast for ever and ever, done in faithfulness and uprightness."

5. **Reward of Sardis:** rest, protection, companionship, and contentment. Psalm 111:9: "He provided redemption for his people; he ordained his covenant forever."

6. **Reward of Philadelphia:** credibility and a name. Psalm 111:9: "Holy and awesome is his name."

7. **Reward of Laodicea:** autonomy to create and lead; sovereignty. Psalm 111:10: "The fear of the Lord is the beginning of wisdom; all who follow his precepts have good understanding. To him belongs eternal praise."

Example 14

Daniel 1

Daniel's Training

1. **Reward of Ephesus:** sense of belonging. King Nebuchadnezzar commissioned an exclusive college of the best and brightest young men from among the Hebrew captives to begin training for service to Babylon.

2. **Reward of Smyrna:** life. This group was provided the best food from the royal table. Some, including Daniel, chose a vegetable-based diet.

3. **Reward of Pergamum:** individual responsibility and worth. Daniel learned language and literature from the Babylonians for three years to prepare for national service.

4. **Reward of Thyatira:** responsibility to the group. Upon completion of training, Daniel was to enter service to the nation of Babylon, on behalf of King Nebuchadnezzar.

5. Reward of Sardis: rest, protection, companionship, and contentment. God caused the chief official in charge of Daniel's training to show favor and sympathy to Daniel. This official protected Daniel, Hananiah, Mishael, and Azariah.

6. Reward of Philadelphia: credibility and a name. Daniel, Hananiah, Mishael, and Azariah distinguished themselves as the best, brightest, and healthiest among their peers.

7. Reward of Laodicea: autonomy to create and lead; sovereignty. Daniel, Hananiah, Mishael, and Azariah were, in fact, so remarkable that the king found no equal to them and retained them for his royal service.

Example 15

Matthew 6

The Lord's Prayer

1. Reward of Ephesus: sense of belonging. Matthew 6:9–10: "Our Father in heaven, hallowed be your name, your kingdom come. Your will be done on earth as it is in heaven."

2. Reward of Smyrna: life. Matthew 6:11: "Give us today our daily bread."

3. Reward of Pergamum: individual responsibility and worth. Matthew 6:12: "Forgive us our debts." (God fulfills the individual role, like Examples 4 and 13.)

4. Reward of Thyatira: responsibility to the group. Matthew 6:12: "As we also have forgiven our debtors." (This is our in-kind responsibility to others.)

5. Reward of Sardis: rest, protection, companionship, and contentment. Matthew 6:13: "And lead us not into temptation, but deliver us from the evil one."

CHAPTER 9

Practical Applications in Suicide Prevention

He who has a *why* to live for can bear with almost any *how.*[70]

—Nietzsche

The US Army and the entire US military have battled suicide in the ranks for the past few years. It is a sad and nebulous thing to combat. The US Army has raised awareness of the suicide problem through training stand-downs, systematically conducting classes, and programs for soldiers. This sets the conditions so that soldiers may seek help or others will recognize risk factors and warning signs in their fellow soldiers.[71] Common points of concern in suicide prevention have their antidote in the biblical method of order.

---

70   Viktor E. Frankl, *Man's Search For Meaning: Revised and Updated* (New York: Washington Square Press, 1984), 97. Emphasis added.

71   *Suicide Awareness Guide for Leaders.* Fort Lauderdale: QuickSeries Publishing, © 2009-2013, 7.

Risk Factors of Suicide

Table 3

Financial Problems	That is the inability to sustain life, the reward of Smyrna.
Disciplinary or legal actions	That is a diminished sense of individual value, the reward of Pergamum.
Loss of close relationships or separation	That is a loss of companionship, the reward of Sardis.
Substance abuse	That is a loss of life or a distancing from life, the reward of Smyrna.
Poor social skills—social isolation	That is a loss of status or significance inside the group, the reward Thyatira.
Poor school performance	That is a loss in individual value, the reward Pergamum.
Severe, prolonged stress perceived as unmanageable	That is a loss of rest, leisure, and space and time to exist in a normal context, the reward of Sardis.
Belief that others will be better off without him or her	That is a loss of sense of belonging, the reward of Ephesus.

Warning Signs of Suicide

Table 4

Noticeable changes in hygiene, eating, or sleeping habits	Diminishing of life, the reward of Smyrna
Decrease in job performance	Individual responsibilities not being met, the reward of Pergamum
Irritability and defensiveness	No longer fits into the group, the reward of Thyatira
Change in mood	No longer fits into the group, the reward of Thyatira
Isolation and withdrawal from social situations	No sense of belonging, the reward of Ephesus
Giving away possessions or suddenly writing a will	A person places little value on his or her own worth and is no longer credible, the reward of Philadelphia

I am not entirely convinced our nation is at war. The military and their families are at war and have been for over a decade. There is a difference. Those who have taken part in multiple deployments have defined their existence in terms of pre-deployment training, deployment, combat operations, redeployment, and post-deployment recovery. The cycle then repeats. The nation as a whole, it seems, has barely looked up to notice what a decade of war shouldered by the same individuals really means.

Jeremiah 6:16 says, "This is what the Lord says: 'Stand at the crossroads and look; ask for the ancient paths, ask where the good way is, and walk in it, and you will find rest for your souls.'" A way to see this verse is to stop and be still. Take notice of what is going on around you. Investigate God's eternal righteousness. Emulate that righteousness. Rest in God's contentment.

While I was in Iraq in 2008, a soldier in a different division than my own but nearby committed suicide directly after he was to report to his commander's office in order to receive non-judicial punishment (NJP) for a misdeed. This suicide was a nadir.

Clearly, this soldier's individual worth was compromised when he received punishment from the very organization in which he received his sense of belonging. If a soldier's home situation is also compromised, this military setting may be the only other sense of belonging he or she possesses.

Commanders are obligated to instill order and discipline in their units. This is not optional, so mature judgment and close monitoring of actions and reactions to significant events such as NJP are critical for everyone involved. Civilian leadership faces similar challenges. These biblical concepts of leadership transcend the context.

Leaders administer punishments with a companion. That companion is a recovery plan of action for an individual to reform and reintegrate the individual back into the unit or team. This combined approach is normally accomplished. This approach maintains the integrity of that essential quality—a sense of belonging—that we can never compromise. We do not leave team members in a potential state of despondency without a coherent support network in place. That is graduate-level leadership.

In the scholarly study "Sense of Belonging: a Vital Mental Health Concept" by Bonnie M. K. Hagerty, *et al*, a sense of belonging is recognized as being an essential component of mental health. God also recognizes this as essential to his natural order. The article highlights the fact that many people do not have meaningful connections to other people. The article reads,

> Psychiatric nurses hear ... statements regularly from clients who are psychotic, depressed, anxious, or suicidal: "I don't fit in anywhere ... I feel so unimportant to anyone ... I'm not part of anything. ..." The impetus for these types of statements has been attributed to a number of psychological concepts, including loneliness, alienation, and hopelessness. However,

upon closer examination such statements appear to reflect a unique phenomenon that has received little attention in the mental health literature, sense of belonging.[72]

A sense of belonging is critical. God built a need for a sense of belonging into the framework of our existence. He offers a sense of belonging to all. We must reciprocate. Think back to King Saul's example of impending chaos in Chapter 2. You cannot get to Laodicea without going to Ephesus first and visiting all the intermediate cities in between in order. You must stay with the program; you must use God's method of order.

The 2012 National Strategy for Suicide Prevention:

> As noted in the Introduction, connectedness to others, including family members, teachers, coworkers, community organizations, and social institutions, has been identified as an important protective factor. These positive relationships can help increase a person's sense of belonging, foster a sense of personal worth, and provide access to sources of support.[73]

Look at the components. *Connectedness and a sense of belonging*—we received these in Ephesus. *Teachers*—we met them in Pergamum when we developed ourselves to be subordinates and leaders. *Co-workers, family, organizations, and social institutions*—we met them and learned how to serve in them in Thyatira. *Protection*—we received that in Sardis. *Personal worth*—we learned that in Pergamum. It was Pergamum's focal point.

The secular community of scholars recognizes many of the exact components Scripture outlines. However, they omit the most essential

---

72   Bonnie M. K. Hagerty, *et al*, "Sense of Belonging: A Vital Mental Health Concept," *Archives of Psychiatric Nursing*, Volume VI, No. 3 (June 1992): 172, accessed February 1, 2013, http://deepblue.lib.umich.edu/bitstream/handle/2027.42/29998/0000365.pdf;jsessionid=A72108C27BC45E9611671A6C664A4E85?sequence=1.

73   US Department of Health and Human Services (HHS) Office of the Surgeon General and National Action Alliance for Suicide Prevention. *2012 National Strategy for Suicide Prevention: Goals and Objectives for Action.* Washington, DC: HHS, September 2012, 35.

point—the starting point. Christ Jesus is the first cause and the originating point of all reference. A sense of belonging through Jesus is the launch pad for life's trajectory.

McMillan and Chavis (1986) raise valid questions that God's method of order answers. These questions answered below are part of the heart and soul of this book. These newly discovered revelations gleaned from the seven churches have laid dormant for millennia until now. The coherence of God's plan for leadership revealed in this book leads the way for us to know God's method and character more intimately. This coherent structure demonstrates God's method of order for leaders to emulate. It also shows how to apply it in the daily relationships that we all have in our organizations. The application of this order in a caring way can save the US Army and other branches of the military from the bane of future suicides in the ranks. "The main point is that people do what serves their needs. But this leaves questions unanswered: How do people prioritize their needs, especially after meeting the basic survival needs? What creates a need beyond that of basic survival?"[74]

God's method of order is the answer! A sense of belonging is surely our foundation. Nothing can replace or mimic it. If we do not possess the reward of Ephesus, then we drift in despondency. It is hopelessness.

The 2012 National Strategy for Suicide Prevention:

> In 2009, the suicide rate among black women aged 20–59 years was 2.77 per 100,000, the lowest rate among adults in this age range. It is possible that factors such as greater social support, larger extended families, and deeper religious views against suicide may help protect some groups from suicide.[75]

---

74 David W. McMillan and David M. Chavis, "Sense of Community: A Definition and Theory," *Journal of Community Psychology* Vol. 14 (January 1986): 13.

75 US Department of Health and Human Services (HHS) Office of the Surgeon General and National Action Alliance for Suicide Prevention. *2012 National Strategy for Suicide Prevention: Goals and Objectives for Action*. Washington, DC: HHS, September 2012, 20.

The salient points from the 2012 NSSP in this demographic are family and religion. These points build and strengthen a sense of belonging in this demographic. Family is God's invention, and practicing true religion can facilitate our sense of belonging to God. In God's method of order, these are foundational concepts that contribute to a sense of belonging.

Scripture substantiates the truth in this statistic and *vice versa*. It is no wonder a demographic strong in foundational components of God's sense of belonging has low suicide rates.

In a military setting, this foundation of a sense of belonging is almost always built in. This concept is baked into the cake. A soldier has a uniform with his or her name on it; his or her name is on the alphabetical alpha roster; and his or her name is on the battle roster according to his or her position, rank, and MOS (military occupational specialty). A soldier has an address. Even if it is the second hole past the third palm tree, a soldier does have an address. This soldier belongs.

The military is normally good at the lesson of Smyrna—the lesson of life. Soldiers are taken care of physically. Commanders, the officer corps, and especially the NCO corps almost never fall down on this job. Soldiers have food, water, time for hygiene as operationally realistic, and shelter. These conditions can be austere and outside the norm of the civilian population, but they are present.

Hygiene is a big indicator of a sense of belonging in a military unit or civilian population. Each one of these aspects of a sense of belonging builds upon the other. Below are two examples of how physiological needs can be leveraged in the context of sense of belonging.

In HM Prison Maze in the late 1970s and early 1980s, the British government held IRA prisoners. It was said the guards severely beat the prisoners when they left their cells to take showers or relieve themselves. All the prisoners banded together and refused to go to the facilities. The insides of their cells became septic. The prisoners maintained their sense of belonging by banding together and collectively resisted the guards and government with the only thing they had left—their sense of life, the lesson of Smyrna. Bobby Sands in this same prison fought his fight with even higher stakes from the lesson of Smyrna when he died in a hunger strike on May 5, 1981. I am not an advocate for either side in that complex issue. I use this example only to point to the strength a sense of belonging can generate in a population and a single individual.

Assigned to the 1st Battalion of the 8th Marine Regiment in the days after combat operations in Operation Desert Storm, those in my unit lived in holes in the ground for months outside Kuwait City. A truck with potable water came by every morning and gave us all the water we wanted as long as we had containers to hold the water. Within a few days, we had scrounged every bucket in the countryside, and we dutifully lined them up in a row, waiting for the water truck every morning. I am sure that Kuwaiti national truck driver must have laughed when we were not looking. It was not exactly a high-tech operation.

We needed that water, because our platoon sergeant lined us up every day to make sure we kept ourselves respectable, well-shaved, and wearing clean uniforms. It did not matter that we lived in holes in the ground. He was a strong leader who instilled order, because he loved us. Our platoon sergeant knew discipline, order, and health (life) were reflected in how we took care of ourselves.

This also helped maintain our sense of belonging and even spun off into giving us jobs to do—gathering buckets and water. That job fostered our sense of individual worth (Pergamum). Even lining us up in a formation, the platoon sergeant helped foster our sense of responsibility to the group (Thyatira). The platoon formed up with the first squad on the front row, second squad on the second row, and third squad on the third row. Everybody had a spot, and there was a hierarchy inside the squad within the lateral lines. Everybody mattered, and it was a very concrete, tangible, and visual way to see the individual matters with respect to the overall team's constitution and operation. Even if jobs are menial, they are important. We also had autonomy to create our home-holes. The only things between an inverted *Taj Mahal* and us were our shovels and time.

You can see how these lessons build upon each other and facilitate the conditions to advance you through all seven phases. Each reward, starting with Laodicea and working backward to the foundational reward of Ephesus, increases in importance and value.

Graphically capturing this concept, I ascribe value in a tiered triangular scale of importance. This graphic demonstrates the value of each reward; this is shown by the amount of stars ascribed for successfully attaining the reward of each city visited. The more important the lesson, the more stars it receives. *The most important lessons are the first lessons.* Each star is worth the same amount of value. You can only acquire stars step-by-step in God's sequential order.

Travelers cannot jump ahead to Philadelphia to get those two stars of credibility when just establishing themselves as competent individuals in Pergamum. What sense would it make in our own lives or career fields to receive recognition as credible entities when just starting to prove our worth as subordinates? Any achievements, recognition, or awards received in that order or context would immediately be recognized as unfounded. That would devalue all previous, current, and future awards received by that authority, from which their sense of belonging is derived. God's order is the right order!

The Twenty-Eight-Star Leadership Model

Leaders can practically use the seven rewards of the Revelation churches in the scheme outlined below. Leaders can develop their teams with these principles, and subordinates can coherently structure their future goals in this context. The twenty-eight-star leadership model portrays our foundation for the sacred responsibility of leaders who are accountable to God for those whom they lead. Remember our verse at the beginning of the book: "Obey your leaders and submit to their authority. They keep watch over you as men who must give an account. Obey them so that their work will be a joy, not a burden, for that would be of no advantage to you" (Hebrews 13:17).

A Biblical Hierarchy of Needs:

The Twenty-Eight-Star Leadership Model

The first lessons are the most important lessons.

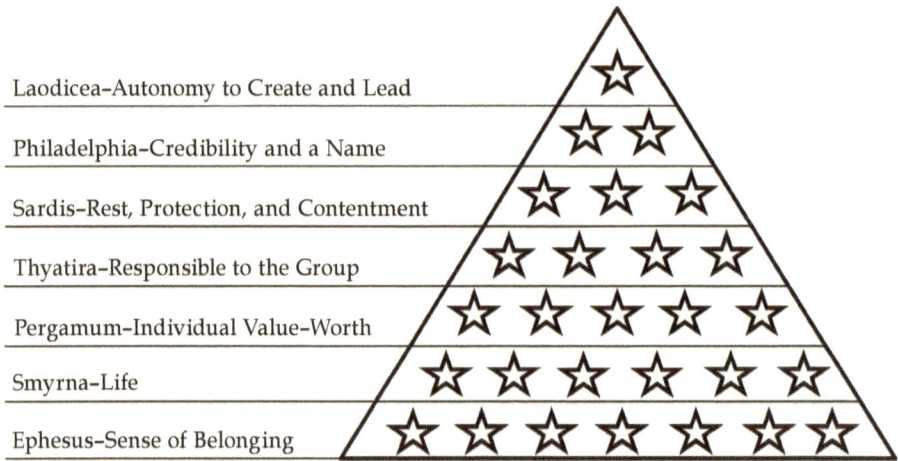

Laodicea–Autonomy to Create and Lead

Philadelphia–Credibility and a Name

Sardis–Rest, Protection, and Contentment

Thyatira–Responsible to the Group

Pergamum–Individual Value–Worth

Smyrna–Life

Ephesus–Sense of Belonging

7 + 6 + 5 + 4 + 3 + 2 + 1 = 28 stars

The biblical hierarchy is simple and true. Other secular hierarchies recognize neither God as holy nor life as sacred. In the biblical hierarchy's base and apex, respectively, God is the source and provides autonomy to create and authority to direct future goals as leaders. In Maslow's hierarchy of needs, people must self-actualize or conjure these qualities. With Maslow's concept, we are on our own.

The twenty-eight-star leadership model leads us to mental rest and resilience via ordered physical work. In the biblical hierarchy, leaders are responsible to God for the development of their subordinates (Hebrews 13:17). Most importantly, in the biblical hierarchy, God is with the traveler (see Chapter 8, Example 3, Sardis). God will help the traveler by directing his or her path (Jeremiah 6:16). It is what he does. This direction is part of his job description as God. He self-advertises as much.

There is a significant stipulation. God is with us unless we reject him. We all have the ability, if not the bent, to alienate God. Faith is the critical starting point in our sense of belonging from God. Faith was one of the first talking points in the city of Ephesus. God is I AM (Exodus 3:14); we only *are*, and so faith *is*. This is the sacred starting point for all we endeavor.

A Leadership Tool

This style of leadership is not my invention. I borrow this method from God. God demonstrates the logic to us in his Scripture. We travelers just have to recognize the method and place it into effect. Two application methods are shown below to aid leaders in practical use of the twenty-eight-star model. Leaders can foster resilience in their subordinates using these models and their associated questions.

The seven rewards of the twenty-eight-star leadership model in practical use:

1.   The group accepts the individual (seven stars).

2.   The individual's physical needs are met (six stars).

3.   The person is unique with individual worth and fulfills his or her responsibilities (five stars).

4.   The individual is relevant to the team and its operational goals (four stars).

5.   The individual has rest through companions, protection, and contentment inside the group (three stars).

6.   The individual has public recognition, by name, as a credible individual with praise and awards (two stars).

7.   The individual functions autonomously in the group with creativity to solve problems and contribute to the direction of the team's future priorities (one star).

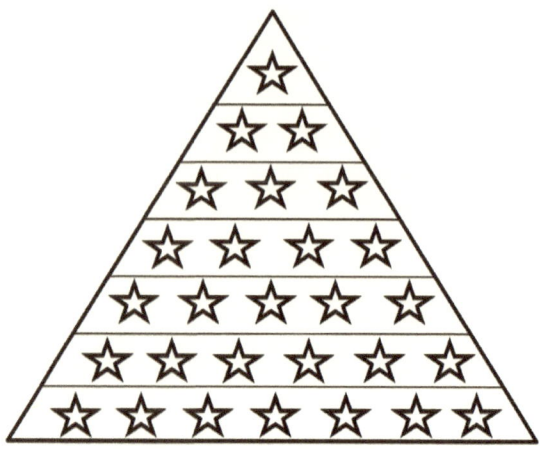

7 + 6 + 5 + 4 + 3 + 2 + 1 = all 28 stars. This is the climate leaders want to create in their organizations. Leaders strive to facilitate this order and purpose for their subordinates.

The Twenty-Eight-Star Mental Checklist

Leaders can use this leadership model to build a mental checklist to help them lead their organizations. They can ask themselves these simple questions to see if they support their subordinates with God's method of order or not. The synergism of these seven questions can facilitate the building of a reciprocating sense of belonging.

1. Did I fully receive and integrate this person into my organization, team, or group?

2. Have I done anything to inhibit the person's ability to sustain himself or herself physiologically?

3. Did I assign this person an appropriate role or job? Is he or she trained for this role or job?

4. Is this person provided opportunities to integrate his or her skills, service, or product into the team in a meaningful way?

5. Is this individual at rest with companionship, protection, and contentment?

6.   Do I recognize this person publically for work accomplished and for work exceptionally accomplished?

7.   Do I reward the most capable individuals with autonomy to lead and direct future organizational goals?

It Is Not One-Sided

The individual has a dog in the hunt, too. A leader cannot facilitate a sense of belonging in an environment with an abrasive, resistant, or unwilling person. Just as Esther listened to Mordecai and Hegai and followed their advice, we also need to have humble attitudes. This will allow others to have meaningful and intelligent conversations with us (see Chapter 8, Example 9). Of course, this has implications in eternal salvation. Jesus asks volunteers to populate heaven. Satan asks volunteers to populate hell. Middle ground does not exist. No traveler just winds up in either place; all tickets are bought freely and consciously (Mark 3:29).

This leadership model advertises the top goal of autonomy. When the time comes, to pass the torch of leadership, there will be qualified and mature personnel to select from.

The Recap

Take a moment to remember how we arrived at this culminating tool—the twenty-eight-star mental checklist.

1.   The Scripture of Ephesus provides the seven-step Ephesus model. The seven steps in that model are the constructs of a sense of belonging. The Ephesus model also became our road map for the journey we just completed. That map led us to the other six rewards in the next six cities.

2.   As the Ephesus model led us to the rewards, we then used those rewards to build the stages of the method of order and the twenty-eight-star leadership model. The twenty-eight-star model is a tool for leaders. It describes the environment or

climate they strive to create for their subordinates to flourish in.

3. The twenty-eight-star leadership model will generate seven questions for the leader and the led. These seven questions comprise the twenty-eight-star mental checklist. This checklist describes the seven practical ways leaders can facilitate a sense of belonging for each person under their sacred responsibility to lead.

This interpretation of the seven churches of Revelation shows us new truths and provides us a new lens through which to view the Bible. The method of order shows us the interconnectedness across the breadth of Scripture and time that no mortal could engineer or even reverse engineer. Since it was only discovered now, how would any biblical writer have known to reverse engineer it, anyway?

The structure of the outline shown through the method of order is embedded throughout Scripture. The outline of the method of order matches the outline of the Ten Commandments. The outline of the Ten Commandments matches the outline of the Lord's Prayer. The outline of the Lord's Prayer matches the story of Ruth and Boaz. The story of Ruth and Boaz follows the outline of Moses' speech to the people in Deuteronomy 28, the Shema, the cultural mandate, Solomon's dedication prayer, the 23rd Psalm, Esther's coronation, etc.[76] The implications of discovering embedded, Spirit-filled links between the Old and New Testaments strengthens the apology of the Messianic position. God's thumbprint is inextricably woven into the fabric of Scripture.

The rewards of the seven churches—the method of order—show us how Jesus leads and develops his church. We, in turn, can borrow his leadership outline, a biblical hierarchy of needs, and make it our own. This hierarchy has application in suicide prevention. The points below are the distilled essence of the seven churches with respect to suicide prevention.

---

76   See Chapter 8.

If a person is …

1.   Accepted (Ephesus)

2.   Physiologically sustained (Smyrna)

3.   Individually relevant (Pergamum)

4.   Plugged into a team with purpose and meaning (Thyatira)

5.   At rest with companionship, protection, and contentment (Sardis)

6.   Publically recognized for competence (Philadelphia)

7.   Given autonomy to direct future goals with creativity (Laodicea)

… then he or she will have a strengthened sense of belonging.

A sense of belonging builds resilience. Resilience is a known protective factor against suicide.

Resilience links to spiritual health. Spiritual health absolutely matters. The 2012 NSSP and US Army leadership recognize this point. The primary utility of the twenty-eight-star leadership model in suicide prevention is to set the spiritual conditions so a person never entertains suicide as a viable option in life (stated in the Introduction). "The Army's charter is more about holistically improving the physical, mental, and spiritual health of our soldiers and their families than solely focusing on suicide prevention. If we do the first, we are convinced that the second will happen," General Peter W. Chiarelli, USA (Ret.).[77]

Although the method of order is newly discovered, it has actually been present in spirit all along. Matthew 22:36–40 teaches us the nerve of the ancient method of order—love God, and love people. Just leadership is an act of worship to the Father. Through leadership, we honor God through honoring his creation.

---

77   *Suicide Awareness Guide for Leaders.* Fort Lauderdale: QuickSeries Publishing, © 2009-2013, 20.

GEN Chiarelli, VCSA, 29 March 2009.

CHAPTER 10

The Comparison

Ultimately, man should not ask what the meaning of his life
is, but rather he must recognize that it is *he* who is asked.[78]

—Viktor E. Frankl

The Biblical Hierarchy versus Secular Hierarchies

The ability of this twenty-eight-star leadership model to assign each
construct a numerical value with percentages and associated analysis
shows a defining difference from Maslow's model. The constructs of
the biblical hierarchy of needs are clearly defined, discrete, unjumbled,
and without overlap. Because of this, we can assign a value to each
course. The system of stars shows the value of each construct. The
most important lessons are the first lessons. Through analysis of the
resulting percentage values, leaders can recognize individuals who
may be in potential peril of suicide.

There are three key differences between the biblical hierarchy and
a secular hierarchy of needs. First, the biblical method starts with
faith to receive a sense of belonging from God. This is the base lesson,
shown as the base of seven stars in the model. Second, at the apex of
the biblical hierarchy, we gain autonomy to lead and create from God

---

78   Viktor E. Frankl, *Man's Search For Meaning: Revised and Updated* (New York:
Washington Square Press, 1984), 131. Emphasis is Frankl's.

(James 4:10). We earn this top reward from our development through gaining the other rewards. It is also given to us through our leaders and employers (Hebrews 13:17). Third, the biblical hierarchy has discrete stages or constructs. Through these specified lines, we can ascribe a numerical value. The method of order supports people whom we are responsible to lead; it cannot culminate in a *me* generation but rather a *team* generation.

If a person has no sense of belonging, he or she will have no stars and therefore be in a very troubled state and possibly at risk of suicide. On the other end of the spectrum, there is a person who has 100 percent of the stars. This individual has methodically matured in God's sequence of development.

Contentment is not rank–or position–dependent. Competence and contentment are not functions of positions. A junior member of a team functioning completely within the scope of his or her influence can achieve all twenty-eight stars. If a private makes autonomous tactical decisions on patrols and has freedom to make suggestions to his team leader or squad leader, he is fully capable in Laodicea. Remember our instruction from Martin Luther; common daily work is God's work.[79] Therefore, the work of the private is equally as valid and needed as the work of the colonel.

At times, even more is needed. In the summer of 2004, my unit conducted combat operations in the mixed Shia-Sunni portions of the Adhamiyah District of northern Baghdad, and we needed a replacement lieutenant (LT). Thinking aloud to the battalion executive officer, I thought that would be a tall order. He told me he could make one phone call and have another LT there by morning, but it would take months to replace a fully qualified rifleman. The rifleman was actually needed more than a LT at that time. Emphasizing the point, the most important people are not always who you might think at first.

---

79   Timothy Keller and Katherine Leary Alsdorf, *Every Good Endeavor: Connecting Your Work to God's Work* (New York: Dutton, 2012), 69–73.

When the private from the previous paragraph is promoted to corporal and later sergeant, he will no longer function at a level commensurate with all twenty-eight stars. This is normal. It will take time to learn a new job. He may find himself at the team level until he becomes more comfortable in this new position. This is how we all progress through the ranks or up the company ladder. We are given greater responsibilities after we demonstrate mastery at the present level.

Our stations, positions, and goals need to be yoked to our capabilities. Otherwise, we may perceive our future positions as being a bridge too far. Leaders may see or sense their subordinates disengage into a circle-the-wagons defensive posture if this attitude creeps in. Leaders need to manage this atmosphere by assigning ability-appropriate goals that develop their teams and team members.

The individual in Laodicea has all the stars. He or she has been to every city in order, and every lesson was built on the last. This is what leaders try to achieve for each individual inside their organization. Leaders train their own replacements, and this model shows the path. This model is not entirely leader-centric. Subordinates can strive to succeed inside the framework of this model as well.

I have partly explained this model in the context of a military unit. That is where I am qualified to speak, and that is where my heart is. Foundations of this leadership model are biblical, and they can work in any context. This method has application in any social setting comprised of leaders and subordinates. God is a leader, and we can borrow his methods. God chose this method to build his own church. He used this style of leadership in the Garden of Eden (see Chapter 8, Example 1). We, in turn, have license, if not obligation, to copy him.

The Breakpoint

Because the twenty-eight-star leadership model's lines are discrete, we can place a numerical value on each course. This chart captures this information.

Table 5

In the first city of	Ephesus	7/28	You gain 25 percent of the stars.
In the second city of	Smyrna	13/28	You gain 46 percent of the stars.
In the third city of	Pergamum	18/28	You gain 64 percent of the stars.
In the fourth city of	Thyatira	22/28	You gain 78 percent of the stars.
In the fifth city of	Sardis	25/28	You gain 89 percent of the stars.
In the sixth city of	Philadelphia	27/28	You gain 96 percent of the stars.
In the seventh city of	Laodicea	28/28	You gain 100 percent of the stars.

To provide some analysis of the chart's meaning and implications, look at the percentage difference between Pergamum to Smyrna. It is a fall from 64 percent to 46 percent. This is an 18 percent point loss, where a person tumbles below the 50 percent mark.

A person in Pergamum has meaning as an individual, but he or she desires full integration into the team. Each person wants the stars of Thyatira. In Thyatira, a person is in a healthy atmosphere, supporting the team in a meaningful and relevant way, but he or she is not content. The stars of contentment (Sardis), credibility (Philadelphia), and autonomy for creative thinking (Laodicea) are still left to gain. There is work to accomplish. Remember, it is no insult to be in Pergamum as long as the individual is developing and trending to a better state. This is normal growth.

Some individuals may be in Thyatira a little longer than necessary. Maybe that could be because they do not have true friends or companions, or they are never at ease in the group because they may have unusual personalities that inhibit their ability to gel with the group. This retarded development could be a function of a team member who is new to the group. It may take more time for the newly assigned team member to feel comfortable in a new setting in order to adjust well. Some people never meet a stranger, and others struggle or require more time to establish meaningful bonds.

This delayed development can also be normal for a person who has an introverted personality type and expends a tremendous amount of energy in a large group setting. Likely, this pause may also be just a normal transitory stopover until building more confidence to emerge as a strong leader later.

If we do not have the reward of Sardis under our belts, then the rewards of Philadelphia and Laodicea automatically are not in our grasps. These rewards are sequential. How can a person's opinion about a future planning priority (reward of Laodicea) matter if he or she has no friendship bonds to rest on (reward of Sardis) or public credibility (reward of Philadelphia)?

Those without true companions will be loners, if not in their physical state, then definitely in an emotional state, to say nothing of their state of professional credibility. How much recognition do you think these people will receive, even though they may be competent individuals? Leaders should always have their antennae up to sense the state of a person's wellbeing. God's method of order will structure what to look for and how to fix what is broken.

Notice that a person in Philadelphia is a competent team member and publically recognized as such but is not at the Laodicea level yet only loses one star. He or she only loses one star! This individual possesses 96 percent of the available stars. A person in Philadelphia may still be developing communication skills. This person may still be developing the skill of organizing his or her ideas into coherent audible suggestions for the team. Regardless, this person functions in a complex environment and is in a good, healthy spot. Further development and positions of authority are likely. When he or she eventually reaches his or her destination in the context of a current assignment, he or she will gain the last 4 percent of the points in the last star.

The relationship of point distribution is not top-heavy; *it is bottom-heavy.* You get more stars for the basic lessons first. The most important lessons and rewards are the first lessons and rewards.

This is good for individuals who develop on schedule. It is doubly bad for individuals who struggle in the middle cities and lose ground. They lose a greater number of stars if their situations deteriorate. Leaders should be cognizant of the fact that this is why, when a person's situation starts going downhill, things seem to accelerate and spiral down quickly. *That is because their situation is spiraling!* The individual is losing control. Chaos encroaches.

King Saul and Judas Iscariot were men in the Bible who committed suicide. King Saul was in a self-induced state of chaos (1 Samuel). This chaos was a function of Saul's own rebellion against God.

The King Saul Example

During a battle that went badly, Saul as king knew he was responsible. Saul was the nation's ultimate authority. He was accountable for this loss on the battlefield. He was also responsible for his earlier decisions that set the conditions for this national defeat.

As tactical formations break down, chaos encroaches. Saul lost the glory, sovereignty, and autonomy that he had in the form of kingship, the reward of Laodicea (minus one star). King Saul also lost his credibility, the reward of Philadelphia (minus two stars). Three of Saul's sons were already killed in this battle. Saul lost his protection as a hostile enemy maneuvered on his position, the reward of Sardis (minus three stars). Because he was king and commander, everyone counted on him. He let his nation and army down. Saul failed the collective team and so forfeited the reward of Thyatira (minus four stars). He fell down on his individual job as king. He lost his self-worth in defeat, the reward of Pergamum (minus five stars). Because of his previous rebellions against the Lord (the root cause of this calamity), his foundational sense of belonging in God, the reward of Ephesus (compromised—seven stars) was already fractured. The prophet Samuel had already confronted him about his departure from God's order. This calamity was all too much for King Saul to bear. He took his own life. Life is the reward of Smyrna (minus six stars). Within minutes, Saul's world collapsed around him.

When the foundational lessons of the twenty-eight-star leadership model fracture, suicide can be the result, as it was in King Saul's case. Notice that King Saul's situation unraveled in reverse order of the coherent order found in the scriptural twenty-eight-star model. The trigger for this unraveling was the compromise of the seven-star foundation. We know God withdrew his spirit from Saul (1 Samuel 16:14) after some episodes during which Saul rebelled against God. These events were clearly factors in the compromise of Saul's foundation in God (his sense of belonging).

Our lessons and rewards are sequential. If we reject God, our undoing can be the same sequence, only in reverse. The foundational course of seven stars in the twenty-eight-star leadership model is non-negotiable. We need God. He is the true and valid foundation. He is the holy agent of first cause in our sense of belonging.

The Judas Iscariot Example

Judas Iscariot also compromised his foundation of seven stars (sense of belonging) when he betrayed Jesus Christ. Judas Iscariot was a thief from the beginning, and Jesus knew it (Luke 22:3–6 and John 6:64–70, 12:6, 13:18). All the other stars of his life were unsupported by a fractured and hollow sense of belonging. The natural result followed.

Judas had a fractured foundation in Christ (the base of seven stars—the most important stars). The other stars then toppled. Judas Iscariot, of his own accord and autonomy, betrayed his leadership role. He devised a diabolical plot against the Lord. He actually led the mob to Jesus (minus one star). His credibility was nil; he was the most notorious traitor of all time (minus two stars). His contentment was forever altered (minus three stars). His responsibility to support the group (Jesus and the other eleven disciples) was also betrayed (minus four stars). He betrayed his training and failed individually (minus five stars). The only thing he had left were the six stars that represent life. But these six stars were unsupported by the essential foundation of seven stars he had already compromised. Judas Iscariot hanged himself as his own twenty-eight-star leadership model collapsed around him because of his diabolic deeds. "May another take his (Judas') place of leadership" (Acts 1:20).

Suicide, of course, is not always the result of misdeeds like these two biblical examples. The causes of suicide are multifaceted, shown by the risk factors and warning signs at the beginning of Chapter 9. Suicide can also be an impulsive act for numerous reasons.

I use these examples only because they are biblical, they highlight the unraveling of the twenty-eight-star leadership model (further proving the validity of the model), and Saul and Judas both had conduct that fractured the seven-star foundation, which was their sense of belonging to God. The loss of this essential foundation of a sense of belonging to God is the first step toward chaos. Ultimately, Saul and Judas separated themselves from God not the other way around.

Leaders can use this leadership model to mitigate disorder in their own organizations. If an employee is not competent or comfortable working inside the team, a supervisor can recognize that as a deficiency in the lesson of Thyatira and mentor the employee on how to integrate his or her individual skills and abilities toward supporting the team. The supervisor can start with simple tasks to build confidence and then increase the difficulty until fully integrated.

The entire time, the leader lets the team see and know that this person is a contributing member and essential for the overall success of the group. This success will facilitate the achievement of the reward of Thyatira. This success at the team level will also create camaraderie that is a reward of Sardis. Then camaraderie will lead the way to credibility and recognition, the reward of Philadelphia. Credible people form the next generation of leaders in an organization, the reward of Laodicea.

If the individual skills are good, then the supervisor automatically knows the employee's sense of belonging inside the context of the team (reward of Ephesus), and his or her physical needs (reward of Smyrna) are adequately met. There may be room to improve each of those aspects, but they are fundamentally met.

Even when a person is odd or unusual socially, a leader can use that to the team's and individual's benefit. I have specialty tools is my toolbox. I may use them only once a year, but when I need that tool, only that tool will do the job. If I try to use the wrong tool in the wrong way, things will not go well. I will have to spend even more money to replace broken parts, etc. People are the same way. One of the joys of leadership is being able to put square pegs in square holes, round pegs in round holes, and even odd-shaped pegs in odd-shaped holes. That is team-building 101.

This true hierarchy of needs has application in our schools. A student who is bullied does not have protection and contentment, the rewards of Sardis. A teacher automatically knows the student will have a compromised sense of credibility among the other students. This is the reward of Philadelphia. The student cannot flourish with respect to the next reward of Laodicea with creativity and autonomy among his or her peers in this setting. In this situation, leaders and teachers must not let the student lose the next sequential reward, the reward of Thyatira. This is the student's ability to contribute meaningfully to the class. A teacher's intervention can keep the dominos from falling by protecting the student's remaining stars.

Leaders must have a bulldog grip on the lesson of Pergamum for each individual person under their care and direction. Leaders must not let an individual fall below this mark. In Pergamum, a person has 64 percent of the available twenty-eight stars. A loss of this reward is an 18 percent point loss to Smyrna. If a person ever thinks he or she is not individually relevant, unique, and no longer even matters to the team, his or her wellbeing falls to only 46 percent of the twenty-eight available stars. *Suicide risk factors and warning signs describe many of those who loiter or backslide into this category.*

Any individual in Pergamum, like King Saul, can ill afford a loss of five of his or her eighteen remaining stars. The next loss, should it occur, is six of only thirteen now available (46 percent). Any loss after this is unthinkable. Imagine how you would react with a similar 18 percent loss in your wellbeing in one critical event and still trending downward.

That is what a backsliding person demoted to Smyrna just went through. Leaders must have situational awareness of the mental states of their subordinates. Leaders must instill meaning through purpose for everyone in their care and fully integrate all individuals into the team. Course corrections are only possible when leaders are physically present and engaged. Mutual respect is an impetus for this style of leadership.

Anyone who has lost individual worth, the reward of Pergamum, may only have life and a sense of belonging remaining. This may or may not be enough for him or her to hold on to, especially if this person does not derive his or her sense of belonging from God.

If adversity comes in this vulnerable state suicide may be the result. People should not loiter or dwell in the city of Pergamum overly long before leaders intervene to advance and mature them. Leaders need to be physically present and in tune with the people in their care. Leaders must provide analysis on potential outcomes, forecasting situations that have historically ended in severe angst or suicide. Suicide risk factors and warning signs advertise critical points to facilitate this forecast.

Many publications list these points in different wording and contexts. I believe that leaders and family can make a difference. Through love, they can inspire hope. Through love, God also inspires hope. I have borrowed God's leadership example to write this book, and we can use his example of love in the same way.

There is one stipulation, though. There is always hope while there is time. Time is the first creation of God, as noted in Genesis 1:1. "In the beginning" are the first three words of the Bible. Apart from time's calibration, there is no beginning. Therefore, time predates its own measurement. Without time, there can be no beginning, so time must be God's first creation.[80]

If there is a beginning, then there is an end implied. Otherwise, why would God start counting in the first place? Time to choose Jesus, God's Son, will not always exist. He is the foundation, and he is where we get our true sense of belonging. Placing our faith in Jesus is step number one.

---

80   Time is God's first creation that we are able to discern through Scripture. Time is a dimension we require for this current existence. It is a component of our current consciousness. Time is temporal—that is to say, its usefulness is temporary.

CHAPTER 11

Method of Order, Now Discovered in the Declaration of Independence

We have done some heavy lifting. For fun, apply the twenty-eight-star leadership model to the Declaration of Independence through sequential excerpts.[81]

1. "We hold these truths to be self-evident that all men are created equal, that they are endowed by their Creator with certain unalienable Rights." *This is a sense of belonging; we were given this in Ephesus (seven stars).*

2. "That among these are Life ..." *Life is the reward we gained in Smyrna (six stars).*

3. "... Liberty and the pursuit of Happiness." *Liberty to be unique, individual worth, and individual responsibility are the rewards we gained in Pergamum (five stars).*

4. "That to secure these rights, Governments are instituted among Men." *We have responsibility to the collective to be*

---

81   National Archives and Records Administration, "Declaration of Independence," accessed June 10, 2013. http://www.archives.gov/exhibits/charters/declaration_transcript.html.

competent subordinates and just leaders; we learned this in Thyatira (four stars).

5. "And for the support of this Declaration, with a firm reliance on the protection of divine Providence, we mutually pledge to each other our Lives, our Fortunes and our sacred Honor." *Companionship, protection, and space to live and grow normally with contentment were received in Sardis (three stars).*

6. The next component of the Declaration of Independence is the signatures—the names. *Philadelphia is about personal credibility, recognition, and making a name for ourselves (two stars).*

7. The Declaration of Independence, upon its issuance, created the United States as an autonomous and sovereign nation. *Laodicea gave us our autonomy to create and a share in the throne of the Lord—a share in his sovereignty (one star).*

$7 + 6 + 5 + 4 + 3 + 2 + 1 = $ all 28 stars in the correct order! The Declaration of Independence plainly reveals the sequential divine method of order, our true hierarchy of needs. Do you think our nation's charter was inspired by God?

POSTSCRIPT

Subsequent Discovery

Matthew 1:1–25

The New Testament opens with the Method of Order.

1. **Reward of Ephesus:** sense of belonging. Matthew 1:1–17 outlines the genealogy of Jesus.

2. **Reward of Smyrna:** life. Matthew 1:18 covers the conception of Jesus.

3. **Reward of Pergamum:** individual responsibility and worth. In Matthew 1:19 Joseph demonstrates his character.

4. **Reward of Thyatira:** responsibility to the group. Matthew 1:20–23 reveals the dream where Joseph receives his instructions to take Mary home as his wife and to accept his role as the earthly father for Jesus.

5. **Reward of Sardis:** rest, protection, companionship, and contentment. In Matthew 1:24 Joseph takes Mary home as his wife.

6. **Reward of Philadelphia:** credibility and a name. In Matthew 1:25 the Christ is born and given his designated name—Jesus.

Works Cited

Bailey, N., Comp. *Dictionarium Britannicum: Or a more compleat Etymological English Dictionary Than any Extant Second Edition.* London: Lamb under the Royal Exchange, 1736.

Barkman, Gregory N. "Addressing Physical Needs," September 23, 2011, MP3 file. Downloaded June 24, 2013. http://www.sermonaudio.com/sermoninfo.asp?SID=92411842393.

Besse, Joseph. *A Full Answer To The Country Parson's Plea Against The Quakers Tythe-Bill, By The Author Of The Replication To The Country Parson's Papers and Plea.* Public Domain Reprint, Originally Printed in London, Printed for T. Cooper, at the Globe, 1736.

Burroughs, Jeremiah. *Rare Jewel of Christian Contentment.* Wilmington: Sovereign Grace Publishers, 1971, 1999.

Cantor, Norman F. *In The Wake Of The Plague: The Black Death And The World It Made.* New York: Free Press, 2001, First Perennial Edition Published 2002.

Eisenhower, Dwight D. *Crusade in Europe.* New York: Doubleday and Company, Inc., 1948.

Elwood, Roger P., Comp. *Great Sermons Volume One.* Uhrichsville: Barbour Publishing, 1998.

Frale, Barbara. *The Templars: A Secret History Revealed.* New York: Arcade, 2009.

Frankl, Viktor E. *Man's Search For Meaning: Revised and Updated*. New York: Washington Square Press, 1984.

Hagerty, Bonnie M. K., Judith Lynch-Sauer, Kathleen L. Patusky, Maria Bouwsema, Peggy Collier. "Sense of Belonging: A Vital Mental Health Concept." *Archives of Psychiatric Nursing* Volume VI, No. 3 (June 1992): 172–177. Accessed February 1, 2013. http://deepblue.lib. umich.edu/bitstream/handle/2027.42/29998/0000365.pdf;jsessionid =A72108C27BC45E9611671A6C664A4E85?sequence=1.

Hayford, Jack W., Ed. *New Spirit Filled Life Bible*, New King James Version. Nashville: Thomas Nelson Inc., 2002.

Helton, John. *The insufficiency of the light of nature: exemplified in the vices and depravity of the heathen world*. London: printed for John and Arthur Arch, and John Wright, 1797.

The Institute of Heraldry. "Shoulder Sleeve Insignia. 39th Infantry Brigade." Accessed February 17, 2013. http://www.tioh.hqda. pentagon.mil/Heraldry/ArmyDUISSICOA/ArmyHeraldryUnit. aspx?u=3663.

Keller, Timothy and Katherine Leary Alsdorf. *Every Good Endeavor: Connecting Your Work to God's Work*. New York: Dutton, 2012.

Kennedy, John F. "Remarks at Amherst College (October 26, 1963)." Accessed June 23, 2013. http://millercenter.org/president/speeches/detail/3379.

Lahaye, Timothy. *Revelation Unveiled*. Grand Rapids: Zondervan, 1999.

Larkin, Clarence. *The Book of Revelation: A Study of The Last Prophetic Book of Holy Scripture, Illustrated*. Philadelphia: Erwin W. Moyer Co. Printers, 1919.

Maslow, A. H. "A Theory of Human Motivation," *Classics in the History of Psychology*. Posted August 2000. http://psychclassics.yorku.ca/Maslow/motivation.htm.

McMillan, David W. and David M. Chavis. "Sense of Community: A Definition and Theory." *Journal of Community Psychology* Vol. 14, (January 1986): 6-23.

Miller, Kathleen. "Military Faces Suicide 'Epidemic,' Panetta Tells Congress." *Bloomberg Businessweek News From Bloomberg*, July 25, 2012. Accessed January 31, 2013. http://www.businessweek.com/news/2012-07-25/military-faces-suicide-epidemic-panetta-tells-u-dot-s-dot-lawmakers.

National Archives and Records Administration. "Declaration of Independence." Accessed June, 10, 2013. http://www.archives.gov/exhibits/charters/declaration_transcript.html.

Nee, Watchman. *Come, Lord Jesus.* New York: Christian Fellowship Publishers. Inc., 1976.

Newport, John P. *The Lion and the Lamb: A Commentary On The Book Of Revelation For Today.* Nashville: Broadman Press, 1986.

Norris, Chuck. *The Official Chuck Norris Fact Book: 101 of Chuck's Favorite Facts and Stories.* Carol Stream: Tyndale House Publishers, Inc., 2009.

The Quest Study Bible, New International Version. Grand Rapids: Zondervan Publishing House, 1994.

Rosenthal, Gilbert S. "Some Are Chosen, All Are Loved." Accessed January 30, 2013. http://www.bc.edu/dam/files/research_sites/cjl/texts/cjrelations/resources/articles/rosenthal.htm.

Roth, Sid. *They Thought For Themselves: Ten amazing Jews.* Shippensburg: Destiny Image Publishers, Inc., 2009.

Suicide Awareness Guide for Leaders. Fort Lauderdale: QuickSeries Publishing, © 2009-2013.

Tuckett, J.D. *A History of the Past and Present State Of The Labouring Population: Including the Progress of Agriculture, Manufacturing and Commerce, Volume One.* London: printed for Longman, Brown, Green And Longmans, and Edward Nettleton, Bookseller, Plymouth, 1846.

US Department of Health and Human Services (HHS) Office of the Surgeon General and National Action Alliance for Suicide Prevention. *2012 National Strategy for Suicide Prevention: Goals and Objectives for Action.* Washington, DC: HHS, September 2012.

Zacharias, Ravi. *In the Course of Human Events.* Norcross: Ravi Zacharias International Ministries. Compact disc, 2010.

www.ingramcontent.com/pod-product-compliance
Lightning Source LLC
Chambersburg PA
CBHW032026290526
45786CB00011B/540